"It's hard to explain what draws a man to a jar of severed fingers. Or a famous toilet. Or a grave site of a president's horse . . . Zurcher (think Charles Kuralt without the mistress scandal) has been zigzagging across the Buckeye State's byways for more than 20 years now and knows just about every oddball statue and down-home museum imaginable."

– Akron Beacon Journal

"Zurcher is like a favorite, joke-telling, fun-loving uncle . . . For *Ohio Oddities* [he] delved even deeper into the strange world of Ohio's kookiest destinations . . . It may be bizarre, but it's true American culture that is also uniquely Ohio."

– Ohio Magazine

"With attractions like these, who says Ohio is just 'fly-over country'? . . . Neil Zurcher, a Cleveland TV personality, made a living out of ferreting out Ohio's biggest, smallest, tallest, fattest, or just really have to dig too deep to find Ohio's wide, wild streak of weirdness."

– The Blade (Toledo)

"Just finished *Ohio Oddities* while on a swing out of town covering stories for CNN. I found it oddly delightful. Those leaning over my shoulder on the airplane felt the same. It's a wonderfully wacky page turner. As a fellow Buckeye it made me proud to see Ohio put the "O" in odd!"

– Martin Savidge, CNN

"This is one of those books that's like eating potato chips. You read one story and you have to keep going . . . *Ohio Oddities* is chock full of great stories and places to visit. Zurcher, as usual, has done his job well."

– Medina County Gazette

"People may act grossed out when they hear about things like pickled human fingers in a jar. But they still love to know about them. Just ask Neil Zurcher . . . The humorous and offbeat more than balance the book's grotesque accounts."

– Chronicle-Telegram

"Compiles all manner of quirky little museums, festivals, historic lore, and natural wonders from around Ohio."

– Athens News

Also by Neil Zurcher:

Strange Tales from Ohio
Ohio Road Trips

A Guide to the Curious Attractions of the Buckeye State

[Second Edition]

Neil Zurcher

GRAY & COMPANY, PUBLISHERS
CLEVELAND

This book is dedicated to my wife, Bonnie
to my kids,
Melody and Ernie McCallister
Melissa and Peter Luttmann
Craig W. Zurcher
to my grandkids,
Allison and Bryan McCallister
Ryan and Jason Luttmann,
and to Lowell Gatts, a teacher, who became my friend, and taught
me to be curious. A man who believed I could achieve things when
others did not. A man who made a difference in young lives, but
whose own life ended much too soon.

© 2008 by Neil Zurcher

Photo credits appear on page 222.

Gray & Company, Publishers
www.grayco.com

Library of Congress Cataloging-in-Publication Data
Zurcher, Neil.
Ohio oddities : a guide to the curious attractions of the Buckeye State
/ Neil Zurcher.—2nd ed.
p. cm.
Includes index.
ISBN 978-1-59851-047-8
1. Ohio—Guidebooks. 2. Ohio—Miscellanea. 3. Curiosities and
wonders—Ohio—Anecdotes. I. Title.
F489.3.Z875 2008
917.7104′44—dc22   2008029136

Printed in the United States of America
10 9 8 7 6 5 4 3 2 1

CONTENTS

INTRODUCTION

When I was very young it was the time of the Great Depression and my family, like lots of families then, was just scraping by. My father was an executive with an insurance company, but with the Depression not many people were buying insurance and we lived with my mother's parents.

For entertainment, we took lots of car rides. My father was always interested in the curious, the unusual. The first trip I recall was to Pymatuning Lake, just across the Pennsylvania border, where people fed day-old bread to the hungry carp. The carp were so numerous that the water would literally boil as thousands of fish would fight for a bread crust tossed from the shore. There were also wild ducks and geese on the lake, and they would try to get into the act too. It was quite a sight, watching ducks and geese literally walk on the backs of the fish as they all competed for the bread.

Then there was the "Blue Hole" in Castalia, Ohio. That one I didn't understand too well when I was very young. All I could see was a pond filled with blue-green water. There were no fish, nothing moved—I thought it was pretty boring. My father assured me that this was a special place because the "hole" had no bottom, that according to early brochures horses and cows had fallen in and never been seen again, sucked into some kind of underground river. Well, that made it a little more interesting, and besides there was a trout stream beside it where you could get a box of popcorn and feed the fish. (We did a lot of fish feeding during those years.)

My father loved to call my attention to the biggest, the smallest, the one-and-only of anything he had seen or read about.

Of all the wild and wonderful curious spots we would seek out my favorite was in Mitawanga, Ohio, west of Vermilion. A man had an electric train set that he had built into his backyard. He called it Miniature City, and it was about the size of half a tennis court. It was a magic place for little kids. The trains ran in and out of real mountains that he had made of dirt. The little river that ran through the town was real water, and the tiny homes had electric lights and real grass lawns. Everything was in perfect scale, including the tiny cannonballs stacked by a miniature Civil War cannon in a park. There were sound effects and music, and for a nickel (or maybe it was a dime), you could stay as long as you wanted. I found it especially magical after dark, when you could walk under the stars and feel like Gulliver discovering the land of the Lilliputians.

As a reporter for nearly half a century, I have had plenty of opportunities to continue discovering wonderful little curiosities around the state—many that might not make the news but did get a scribble in the back of my reporter's notebook to remind me that someday I should visit them again and perhaps tell their story.

I don't think that any one section of Ohio has claim to being the oddest part of the state. I'm sure that there will be more things listed here from the northern part of Ohio because that's where I live, and I've been exposed to more things here. But I have been traveling Ohio, all of Ohio, for my "One Tank Trips" television segments for more than 25 years, and also writing about it for the auto club's *Ohio Motorist* magazine and twice monthly for the Cleveland *Plain Dealer*, and I've learned that the odd can be found almost anyplace. Strange is no stranger to Ohio. From a baseball thrown from outer space to start a World Series baseball game in Cleveland to a museum in Marietta where they feed fish with baby bottles, to a wacky field of six-foot-tall cement ears of corn near Columbus, no matter where you live in our wonderful state, you will find idiosyncrasies, curiosities, and oddities. I hope that perhaps this book will "prime the well" and that you'll let me know about things I may have missed so that every couple of years I can bring this book up to date with more of the wondrous and weird things that make the Buckeye State such an interesting place.

OHiO
Oddities ™

CENTRAL
OHIO

The First Traffic Light

The next time you zip through a red light, you might remember a couple of Ohioans who were responsible for that signal.

Garrett A. Morgan, of Cleveland, was the first person to apply to the U.S. Patent Office for a patent on such a device. Morgan's worked this way. It was a T-shaped pole unit that featured three positions: stop, go, and an all-directional stop position. The third position was used to allow pedestrians to cross safely. While technically not a light, this traffic signal led to further inventions.

Teddy Boor, of Ashville, invented and built the nation's oldest working traffic *light*. It was installed in downtown Ashville, south of Columbus. This odd-looking unit offered red and green lights with a slowly rotating hand that would sweep across each bulb, letting drivers know how much time was left before the light would change. The bullet-shaped light hung at the corner of Main Street and Long Street for more than 50 years, until finally the state transportation department made the community take it down and replace it with a more modern signal.

The village obeyed, but saved their piece of history in the **Ashville Museum** (34 Long St., Ashville; 740-983-9864), where it still stops and starts visitors.

The Chicken Who Bought His Own Lunch

ASHVILLE

In Ashville, they still talk about the chicken who bought his own lunch. His name was Chic-Chic, and as chickens go he was pretty small. Actually, he was a bantam rooster, which means that even full grown he barely topped six inches from his feet to the top of his rooster comb. But Chic-Chic was a giant in his own mind.

He belonged to a local widow, who lived just around the corner from a restaurant. Every day the woman would put a dime in Chic-Chic's beak and tell him to go to the restaurant and get his food.

The little bird, dime clenched tightly in his beak, would strut down to the corner, make a left on Long Street, and continue strutting right down the middle of the sidewalk, forcing humans to give way as he made his way to the front step of the restaurant. There he would deposit the dime and stand, clucking, until the owner brought out a Ball jar cap filled with corn and set it down for Chic-Chic to eat from.

Jack Lemon, a volunteer at the Ashville Museum, remembers Chic-Chic well. "That little bird would make that trip every day, winter or summer, rain or shine," he said.

And when he was done eating, Chic-Chic would wander over to the bus stop to greet visitors from other towns. No one knew how he did it, but he always seemed to know just when a bus was due, and he would be there to cluck at the arrivals.

"He just thought he owned this town" former mayor and now museum curator Charlie Morrison told me. "Everybody knew him, everybody loved him."

Today Chic-Chic and his owner are gone. (Chic-Chic died back in the 1950s), but there's a model of the little guy, with a dime in his beak, in the **Ashville Museum** (34 Long St., Ashville; 740-983-9864).

One Speedy Pumpkin Carver
BALTIMORE

Jerry Ayers of Baltimore, Ohio, is not a man to trifle with when he has a knife in his hand. He can carve up a face in literally seconds.

Jerry, you see, is one of the world's fastest pumpkin carvers.

It wasn't a lifelong goal. Jerry was once a real-estate salesman, but his hobby of carving pumpkins for his kids and grandkids kept getting in the way.

Jerry found that by designing his own carving knife, with a long thin blade, he could carve out the face of a jack-o'-lantern faster than anyone he knew. When TV station WCMH in Columbus challenged him to carve a pumpkin on their live show one morning, he took the challenge and set an unofficial world record—1 minute and 56 seconds! And it wasn't your normal saw-toothed, triangle-eyed jack-o'-lantern—it was a series of graceful swirls and arches that created a face with eyes and eyebrows, a distinctive nose, and a mouth that was a work of art. Jerry had found a new career.

In 1999, he entered the *Guinness Book of World Records* as the world's fastest pumpkin carver. He carved a "very detailed jack-o'-lantern" in 1 minute and 37 seconds. On the day he set that record, he set a second one by carving more than a ton of pumpkins in just 7 hours and 11 minutes. The following year he broke his own single-pumpkin record with a time of 1 minute and 18 seconds in an appearance on CBS's *Saturday Early Show* in New York.

Jerry now sells his knives and his pumpkin face designs under the name of "Designer Pumpkins" in grocery stores all over the country and on the Internet. And he still carves his own jack-o'-lanterns each Halloween at his home in Baltimore.

The Greatest Pumpkin
CIRCLEVILLE

EVENTS!

Linus should have looked for The Great Pumpkin in the town of Circleville, home to the "Greatest Free Show on Earth"—the **Circleville Pumpkin Show**, always held on the third weekend in October.

And they like their pumpkins big. One first-prize winner weighed 1,528½ pounds!

The festival started in 1903, when mayor George R. Haswell decided to hold a small exhibit for Halloween in front of his

place on West Main Street. Some corn fodder and carved pumpkins were the decorations. People liked it so much that the following year some merchants added more pumpkins to the exhibit, and it slowly grew into an annual event.

They decided to call it the "Greatest Free Show on Earth." The free part is accurate, at least, because no admission fees are charged. Over the years the show has grown to the sixth-largest festival in the United States and attracts upward of 300,000 people for its annual four-day run.

Today at the festival you can find not only pumpkins but also anything you can name that is made with pumpkin, from pumpkin pie to pumpkin cookies and pumpkin ice cream. There are parades and beauty contests. For four days in the autumn, pumpkins put Circleville on the map.

Bloodletting and Barbering

CANAL WINCHESTER

Barbering has come a long way in the last two centuries. Even into the 1800s, barbers doubled as doctors, doing surgery and also bloodletting with leeches and knives. In fact, the gaily striped barber pole that symbolizes barbering today originally represented the bandages and blood and served as a sign of the barber's ability to do bloodletting. You can learn all the bloody, fascinating history in Canal Winchester, where Ed Jeffers started a barber museum and hall of fame. It's located upstairs from Zeke's Barber Shop (**Ed Jeffers Barber Museum**, 2½ S. High St., Canal Winchester; 614-833-9931). Here you'll find 58 different kinds of barber poles and barber chairs from six generations of barbers. In all, the exhibit covers 150 years of barbering. It's open by appointment only, but if Ed's around you'll get a fascinating tour and learn a whole lot about the field of barbering.

A Painting Comes to Life

COLUMBUS

Is it a garden or a picture? Life imitates art imitating life at a park in Columbus, where sculptor James T. Mason created a living replica of Georges Seurat's famous painting *A Sunday Afternoon on the Island of La Grande Jatte* from plants.

Mason got the idea while visiting a botanical garden in Philadelphia where, he said, the gardens and topiaries reminded him of an impressionist painting.

He came back to Columbus and turned the **Old Deaf School Park** at East Town and Washington Avenue into a living copy of Seurat's masterpiece.

The park now contains 80 life-size topiaries that depict Parisians dressed in their Victorian-era clothing looking at the river Seine.

Mason has created art with yew trees that he trims and shapes

to match life-size molds of the figures he wants. The garden painting includes human figures, a boat being rowed on a pond, and three dogs, a cat, and a monkey.

Admission to the park, located only blocks from the Ohio Statehouse, is free.

The Accounting Hall of Fame

COLUMBUS

Who can forget the glory days of Joel Stanley Demski, Shaun Fenton O'Malley, or Ross Macgregor Skinner?

These and other greats are enshrined at Ohio State University. Are they football players, you ask. Baseball stars? Nope. Accountants.

Yes, OSU is home to the **Accounting Hall of Fame** (Fisher College of Business, Ohio State University, 2100 Neil Ave.,

Columbus; 614-292-9368). It was established in 1950 "for the purpose of honoring accountants who have made, or are making, significant contributions to the advancement of accounting since the beginning of the 20th century."

More than 60 number crunchers have been enshrined. No parades or big hoopla when new members enter, though: just the presentation of a certificate at the annual meeting of the American Accounting Association.

I think the Accounting Hall of Fame should have a gift shop where visitors and accounting fans could go to buy, say, T-shirts with a picture of a ledger book on them, or perhaps with some snappy columnar entries as a graphic. Coffee mugs with . . . well you get the idea.

Which Came First, the Whistle or the Pea?

COLUMBUS

The last of its breed, the **American Whistle Corporation** (6540 Huntley Rd., Columbus; 877-876-2380) is the only maker of metal whistles in the United States.

Whistles. You know. Those things that policemen use. Referees and coaches clench them tightly in their jaws. Majorettes and drum majors use them to command bands and flag corps. In fact, the company makes the official NFL referee whistles for the annual Super Bowl game.

If you want to see how they make whistles (the big moment is when they squeeze in the little ball of cork), they'll show you around for a fee that includes a whistle when you leave. (They'll then trot you through the company store, where you can buy a commemorative bronze, gold, or silver whistle to present to your favorite coach or policeman.)

Butter Cows
COLUMBUS

EVENTS!

Rodin was famous for *The Thinker*, Michelangelo for his *David*. Dan Ross of Columbus is known for his cow made of butter. He started sculpting the cow in 1963 and created a new one each year for the next 36 years.

The first time I went to the Ohio State Fair I was only 14 years old, but I knew there was one thing I wanted to see. Not the Grand Champion bull. Not the horse-pulling championship. Not the Hollywood stage show. No, what I wanted to see first was the life-size cow made of butter.

I had been hearing about this cow since I was old enough to remember. My grandmother had gone to the state fair, and her most vivid memory was of a man using buckets of warm butter to mold a dandelion-yellow Holstein. No little bitty statuette; this was a full five-foot-tall, six-foot-long cow, right down to the faucets in the back. I figured if it was good enough to impress Grandma, I should see it, too.

I walked into a big hallway, and at the end was a frosted-over window looking into a giant refrigerator. There she was. And not only a life-size butter cow, she also had a life-size, Grade-A butter calf right alongside her. It was the most curious thing I had ever seen. I was disappointed later to find out that state fairs in other states have also displayed cows made of butter. But how many of them have also displayed Neil Armstrong, John Glenn, and race-car driver Bobby Rahal in 1,500 pounds of butter?

The cow and calf are still featured each year at the **Ohio State Fair** (17th St., Columbus; 888-646-3976).

Down the Drain Hall of Fame

COLUMBUS

Just about every career has a hall of fame. At least it seems that way in Ohio, where we have the Accounting Hall of Fame as well as the better-known Pro Football Hall of Fame and Rock and Roll Hall of Fame. We're also home to a hall of fame concerned with excellence in getting things to go down the drain.

The **International Drainage Hall of Fame** (590 Woody Hayes Dr., Columbus; 614-292-2011) is located at Ohio State University in Columbus. Its enshrinees include professors, contractors, engineers, and drainage consultants who, I would guess, have made outstanding contributions to the world of agricultural drainage.

The hall of fame is located in the lobby of the Agricultural Engineering Building at OSU, where plaques honoring the inductees line the walls of the lobby.

What's "Brushstrokes" Got to Do with Flying?

COLUMBUS

During the 1970s, "Pop Art" was all the rage, and the icon of the era was Roy Lichtenstein. By the mid 1980s, the Columbus city council was ready to show they were "with it" and commissioned Lichtenstein to create a modernistic abstract piece for the **Port Columbus Airport** (4600 International Gateway, Columbus; 614-239-4083).

Lichtenstein delivered *Brushstrokes in Flight*, a 25-foot-tall, angular aluminum sculpture with what appear to be giant brush strokes soaring into the sky.

The commissioners were apparently less than overwhelmed by the artwork; they put it in the airport's daily parking lot, where it was spattered by rain, dust, and dirt for many years, with hardly anyone noticing its existence.

In fact, at one point then-mayor Dana "Buck" Rinehart tried to give the sculpture away. He offered it to Columbus's sister city, Genoa, Italy. Maybe Buck just hated the sculpture and wanted it far away from Columbus; maybe he really liked it and was trying to make a big impression with his grandiose offer. Either way, he forgot to ask City Council, which reminded him it was city property and not his to give away. (The fact that at about that time the sculpture was appraised at $750,000 may have had something to do with their decision to keep it.)

The commissioners finally moved the statue out of the weather and inside the terminal to a more dignified location—near the food court. They even built a bench around it to keep kids from climbing on it.

The Ghost in the Observatory

DELAWARE

The **Perkins Observatory** (Ohio Wesleyan University, 257 E. Broad St., Delaware; 740-363-1257) in Delaware has the second-largest telescope in the state of Ohio. And a ghost.

The ghost is Hiram Mills Perkins, who was a professor of mathematics and astronomy at Ohio Wesleyan from 1857 to 1907. Perkins loved the stars and was obsessed with someday building an observatory to study the cosmos. It is claimed that he wore the same suit every day for 10 years as part of his plan to save money to build an observatory. During the Civil War, he took a leave of absence to raise pigs to sell to the Union forces. The money he raised from that venture, and his frugal ways, enabled him to save up $250,000. He presented the money to the university in 1923, with the stipulation that they build an observatory of the "first magnitude." Sadly, he died before the building was completed.

Down through the years there have been reports of an old man who appears in the dome sometimes late at night and just watches as people line up to peer through the telescope. Some say it's the ghost of Hiram Perkins just checking up on his observatory.

GENTLEMEN, START YOUR, UH ... LAWN MOWERS

COLUMBUS

It started in 1991 with a one-dollar bet between two residents of Dewberry Lane in Columbus who decided to race each other while mowing an elderly neighbor's lawn. The bet was on whose riding mower could get through a swampy part of the lawn the fastest. This was the start of the "Pit," and the formation of the Dewberry Mudboggers Lawnmower Racing Team—the world's only known lawn mower mud-racing team.

The venerable sport of lawn mower racing has, of course, mowed its way across America. Though there's some disagreement about how and exactly where it started, it was probably in some suburban subdivision, the kind with the big lawns, that just screams for a riding mower. Anyone who has ever chugged up and down a big lawn on top of one of these mini-tractors knows how boring it can be. I suspect two neighbors just found a way to beat the boredom.

Though today there are hundreds of lawn mower racers across America, to my knowledge the only "lawn mower mud racers" are Ohioans—the Dewberry Mudboggers Lawnmower Racing Team. Their motto? "We just love to kick grass!"

The Big Ear

DELAWARE

Did E.T. try to call Ohio back in 1977 and we didn't answer? There's evidence that he or one of his extraterrestrial buddies did, but we didn't know how to reply.

It's gone now, but the "Big Ear" was our listening post in Ohio—for any sign of, or communication from, extraterrestrial intelligence.

The Big Ear was a project of The Ohio State University and was the longest-running SETI (Search for Extra Terrestrial Intelligence) project ever conducted. It lasted from 1973 to 1998.

The "Ear" was a Kraus-type radio telescope that covered an area larger than three football fields. During its watch on the heavens it became famous for sighting some of the most distant known objects in the universe. It also received the "Wow" signal.

The "Wow" was an especially strong signal picked up in 1977 that bore all the earmarks of being extraterrestrial. It was called "Wow" because of a comment penciled in the margins of a computer print-

No, it's not your old electric football game. This model of the "Big Ear" is all that's left of an ambitious interstellar answering machine.

out by Jerry Ehman, one of the scientists who was working on the project. The signal was at least one lunar distance away from Earth at a time when no known satellites were near the source.

But even the demolition of Big Ear doesn't mean that we quit listening. OSU is now in the process of designing and building a next-generation radio telescope called "Argus."

The Perkins Observatory (Ohio Wesleyan University, 257 E. Broad St., Delaware; 740-363-1257) has a small exhibit about the Big Ear, as well as the original computer printout from the day the "Wow" signal was heard and a model and pictures of the Big Ear.

More Big Ears

DUBLIN

Ohio is noted for its corn. Field corn, sweet corn—why, by late summer the state is a veritable cornucopia of ears bursting from their stalks. But Dublin is the only place in Ohio where the corn is on the stalk year 'round.

The Dublin Arts Council sponsored a program called "Art in Public Places," and one of the sculptures—*Field of Corn (with Osage Orange Tress)*—looks like some farmer's dreamscape. Rows and rows of human-sized corn—109 ears in all—stand upright like some kind of denuded carousel in front of a treeline of (you guessed it) Osage orange trees. The sculpture was created by Columbus artist Malcolm Cochran in 1994. The concrete corn was cast in three different sizes to approximate the size of various humans.

The corn is supposed to celebrate Dublin's history as a farming community and to serve as a memorial to rural landscapes that have been consumed by urban development. Fittingly, it's located at **Sam and Eulalia Frantz Park** (4995 Rings Rd., Dublin), a former field that belonged to a pioneer in the agriculture world who specialized in creating different kinds of corn hybrids.

This is just one of several large sculptures the Dublin Arts Council has sponsored. In **Scioto Park** (7377 Riverside Dr., Dublin) is a tribute to Leatherlips, a Wyandot Indian chief. Made of pieces of limestone, it resembles a downsized sphinx. (If you stand on top of Leatherlips's head, you have a ringside seat for whatever is playing at a nearby amphitheater.)

Brutus Buckeye
COLUMBUS

Ohio State University's football mascot is a nut.

I don't mean that the person who serves as mascot is deranged. The mascot itself, Brutus Buckeye, is a nut.

In fact, all of us who live in Ohio are nuts, because we're all called "Buckeyes."

A buckeye is a large, rather useless nut that grows on a tree. Humans can't eat it and so far have found little use for it. My grandfather said "pigs won't even eat buckeyes." (He tried without success during the Great Depression.)

The name reportedly originated on September 2, 1788, at the first court of record of what was then the Northwest Territory. Colonel Ebenezer Sproat, who headed up the court, was greeted by Native Americans shouting what sounded like "hetuck, hetuck, hetuck." It supposedly translated as "eye of the buck," and the judge took it as a compliment. (Humorists have claimed that the Indians were actually not saying "hetuck," but, "he-ugly.") Evengually Ohioans began calling themselves "Buckeyes," too—after the native tree whose nut also looks like the "eye of a buck."

Now, just "Bucks" would be a lovable nickname and mascot. Why not "Ohio State Bucks"? It brings to mind a king-of-the-forest stag and suggests pride and leadership. What does a nut offer? Our neighbors from Michigan are called the "Wolverines." Now, that's a tough, crafty animal you don't want to mess with. About the only danger from a buckeye is if it should fall from the tree and hit you in the head.

At least the state symbol OSU used wasn't the state insect. I don't think I would like to be known as a "Ladybug." And, let's face it, those football players would look strange running around in polka dots.

Arnold Schwarzenegger's Tank

GROVEPORT

What is California governor and movie actor Arnold Schwarzenegger's army tank doing in a Columbus, Ohio, suburb?

Years ago Warren Motts of Groveport, Ohio, started a small Civil War collection in his home that eventually grew into a huge, state-of-the-art military museum.

Warren is a very determined man when it comes to **the Motts Military Museum** (5075 S. Hamilton Rd., Groveport; 614-836-1500; closed on Mondays).

His interest in historic military items began with a Civil War sword that he bought at a flea market and has grown from a private collection in his basement into one of Ohio's finest military museums with hundreds of exhibits.

The particular tank in question is one that actor-governor Schwarzenegger drove when he served in the Austrian army in the 1960s. It's a U.S. model M-47 used by American forces during the Korean War and later by NATO soldiers. It now belongs to Schwarzenegger, who obtained it from the Austrian government. He has given Warren Motts a long-term loan of the totally restored vehicle.

Motts first spotted the tank when Schwarzenegger had it shipped to Columbus for the grand opening of a Planet Hollywood restaurant, one of a chain of which Schwarzenegger is part owner. Motts started a letter-writing campaign to Schwarzenegger's Hollywood office, offering to give the tank a good home at his museum. He kept up the correspondence until one day Schwarzenegger's attorney showed up at the museum. He looked over the place, liked what he saw, and a short time later the tank arrived. Since then, Governor Schwarzenegger has been a fairly frequent visitor at the museum, occasionally taking a short drive in his tank around the museum grounds for old time's sake.

"He's a very personable guy," says Warren Motts, "and he sure thinks a lot of that tank. It's one of his prized possessions. We're grateful to have it here."

But the museum is not about Arnold Schwarzenegger. Wandering around the grounds you find a self-propelled howitzer from the Vietnam War, a Higgins landing craft from World War II, and an exact replica of the boyhood home of Columbus native and World War I flying ace Captain Eddie Rickenbacker. The Rickenbacker family has donated many items that will be displayed in the home.

In the museum building there is a corncob pipe once owned by General Douglas MacArthur. In another display case is the field uniform of Vietnam War General William Westmoreland. How did Motts get these items? "I just asked for them and they gave them to me," he said.

Even Iraqi badman Saddam Hussein succumbed to Motts's persistence. There is a display case with a huge Iraqi flag and two ornately framed pictures of the former Iraqi leader. "I'm no fan of his," Motts explains, "but he is a part of history."

Motts started writing Hussein right after the first Gulf War, asking for a flag or a picture to put in the museum. He heard nothing for years, but after repeated requests, just before U.S. forces toppled the Iraqi strongman, Motts got a call from the Iraqi embassy in Washington informing him that a gift from Hussein was on the way. It turned out to be the flag and two pictures.

"Sometimes you just have to keep asking," Motts said with a grin.

His board of directors includes several well-known veterans, including General Paul Tibbits, also of Columbus, who was the pilot of the Enola Gay, the B-29 that dropped the first atomic bomb on Hiroshima in 1945, which, some say, finally ended World War II. Another board member is Captain Harold Sawyer, one of the original Tuskegee Airmen.

But getting back to the Schwarzenegger tank, I asked Warren Motts what the California governor told him the last time he visited the museum.

Motts smiled, and in an impersonation of the California governor he said, "I'll be back."

Who Really Said . . .

MARION

"Ask not what your country can do for you. Ask what you can do for your country." The famous quotation from John F. Kennedy's inauguration speech still reverberates through the years as a challenge to all Americans. But did he possibly borrow the quotation from another United States president?

Back on June 7, 1916, Senator Warren G. Harding of Ohio brought the Republican national convention to its feet with a real "stem-winder" of a speech. The Republicans went on to lose the presidency that year, but four years later a war-weary nation turned to the man who had made a good impression in 1916, and Harding was elected president

The Harding Home (380 Mt. Vernon Ave, Marion; 800-600-6894) still stands just as Harding left it in 1920 to go off to the White House. There, on a small monument in the rose garden, a few lines from that speech are inscribed: "We must have a citizenship less concerned about what the government can do for it . . . and more concerned about what it can do for the nation." It does have a familiar ring, though not quite as snappy as Kennedy's version.

And to be fair, Harding's own inaugural speech wasn't so captivating. (He promised a "return to normalcy.")

The Peripatetic Monument

MARION

Do you love a mystery? They have a real doozy in Marion. There is a cemetery marker that will not stay still. It's been moving for more than a hundred years.

It all started back in the 1880s when the Charles Merchant family marker was placed in the Marion Cemetery (630 Delaware Ave.). It was a large block of white granite, topped by an orb of solid black granite weighing more than five tons.

Two years after the ball was placed in the cemetery, workers realized that it had moved.

The unpolished base of the round granite ball was now on the side of the ball instead of underneath it. Workers got a crane and, with much effort, returned the ball to its upright position with the unpolished circle on the bottom. To insure that it did not wander again, they put a lead seal around the bottom. "That should keep the monument still for eternity," one of the workmen said.

Wrong.

Hold on tight! The mysterious five-ton Merchant family marker in Marion won't sit still for anyone.

Within a short time the ball began to rotate again. It's been over a century now, and the ball still moves at the rate of about an inch a month.

Such luminaries as radio broadcaster Paul Harvey and Robert Ripley of *Believe It Or Not* fame have investigated the roving ball, as have scientists from as far away as Russia. They have offered theories about moving mass, about heat and cold causing contractions in stone. They all sound very good, except they fail to answer one other mystery about the stone. The ball rests against the bottom stone: if it were moved, it would be scratched. But there are no scratches. It is as though a giant hand picks the stone up and gently turns it slightly. And there is a similar ball and pedestal in another part of the cemetery that has not moved even a fraction of an inch in the last century.

The moving monument has become such a tourist attraction that it is included in bus tours of the city. For more information contact the **Marion Area Convention and Visitors' Bureau** (1952 Marion-Mt. Gilead Rd., Marion; 800-371-6688).

Napoleon's Horse

MARION

Prince Imperial, a huge white Percheron horse born in the stables of Napoleon III of France in 1865, wound up a local celebrity in Marion, Ohio.

Somehow local farmer Jacob Howser found out that the horse was for sale. He went to France, bought the animal, and imported him to the United States in 1868.

Mr. Howser believed in never cutting the horse's mane or tail, and they grew to huge lengths. He also apparently had a bit of the showman in him, since he spent a lot of time showing the horse at county and state fairs throughout the Midwest. It's reported that he would house the horse in a tent and charge a dime to see "Napoleon's horse."

This worked pretty well and probably made Mr. Howser quite a few bucks for about 30 years. Alas, Prince Imperial eventually got old, and in 1890 he died.

Howser, businessman that he was, didn't let a little thing like death get in the way. He simply shipped the dead horse off to a taxidermist and had him stuffed, then continued to cart him from fair to fair. Come to think of it, he probably saved money. He didn't have to buy any more hay or oats.

Prince Imperial, with his long, flowing mane and tail, continued to be an attraction well into the 20th century, when he was finally retired and eventually donated to the Marion County Historical Society, and he can still be seen at **Heritage Hall** (169 E. Church St., Marion; 614-387-4255).

Prince Imperial today (right) and as he appeared back in the early days of the 20th century (left). I guess you don't change much after you're stuffed.

Buckeye Chuck, the Weather Rodent

MARION

Yeah, I know, Punxsutawney Phil was first. The Pennsylvania groundhog gets lots of publicity every year. But Ohio's resident groundhog, Buckeye Chuck, also gets some recognition from the national media each groundhog day.

Chuck got his start years ago when Charley Evers of Marion was working at radio station WMRN. Evers's office faced a nearby woods, and one day he noticed a groundhog hole at the edge of the woods. He started telling his audience about the antics of "Buckeye Chuck," as he named the little groundhog who lived there.

Evers noticed that Buckeye Chuck never came out of his hole during February. (To determine this, he placed a white rag on a stick and put it in the mouth of the hole so that Chuck would have to knock it over to get out.) Chuck usually popped out after the first few warm days in March.

Evers suspected that perhaps Punxsutawney Phil didn't always come out on cue either. State wildlife experts told him that groundhogs usually hibernate all winter, and if you took a sleepy groundhog out of his den in the middle of February, he darn sure wouldn't look for his shadow; he'd head right back for his hole.

National media began to hear of Buckeye Chuck and started calling Evers to see if Chuck had seen his shadow or not. Depending on Evers's mood he would assure them that the little fellow had seen his shadow and darted back into the hole, or he might say it was a cloudy day and Chuck saw nothing before running back in his den.

But then the TV reporters started arriving, expecting to see a groundhog. Charley leveled with them and pointed to the empty hole. They would set up all day on February 2 taking pictures of Chuck's hole, waiting for him to appear. After one team harangued the town of Marion because their camera crew had wasted a whole day and hadn't seen a groundhog, Charley and his crew decided to make sure it didn't happen again.

They borrowed a groundhog from a local trapper as a stand-in for Buckeye Chuck. Evers was pretty nervous when they released the little guy from his cage because the groundhog had a rather nasty personality. "I was afraid he was going to bite someone," he admitted. The next year they tried a stuffed groundhog from the local taxidermist, to avoid the possibility of a local TV personality getting his finger bitten off.

That didn't play well either. The big-city media started saying unkind things about Buckeye Chuck.

Then Evers had an inspiration. He contacted state wildlife officials and learned that they had this cute little woodchuck, very tame, that they used for wildlife programs in Columbus. Could Evers borrow him on February 2? Absolutely. So ever since, Buckeye Chuck arrives in Marion on February 2 in the keeping of his handler from the state wildlife division. He plods around in front of the cameras, lets reporters poke microphones and cameras at him until they have had their fill, and then he goes back to Columbus in a car to sleep the rest of the winter away.

Shortly after this tradition started, Steve Stewart, then an executive with WMRN, realized what a publicity bonanza Buckeye Chuck was and, with Charley Evers, convinced a local state representative to sponsor a bill making Buckeye Chuck the state's official groundhog.

If you would like to see Buckeye Chuck, just head for Marion on February 2. Rain or shine, Chuck will be there.

OHIO'S HIDDEN PARK

NEWARK

Most Ohioans have never heard of it. In fact, it really doesn't exist anymore. Baughman Park is now just a collection of one man's artwork sprinkled across an overgrown woods in central Ohio.

There are statues of U.S. presidents—McKinley, Lincoln, and Washington. There are carved eagles, bas-reliefs of Native Americans, and famous generals like Ulysses S. Grant. Vandals have taken their toll: a statue of a World War I doughboy is headless, as is the statue of General William T. Sherman.

The park is even listed in the National Register of Historic Places, yet few people have seen it in recent years.

That's because of its location. It sits on a hill overlooking the giant Longaberger homestead and factory campuses where State Routes 16 and 586 come together. The property was purchased by the late basket mogul Dave Longaberger, but he didn't know quite what to do with it.

Company spokesmen say they are still not sure what the future of Baughman Park will be.

Brice Baughman was a teenager when he started carving faces and things into the outcroppings of sandstone on his father's farm. Part of the farm was a quarry, and Brice learned how to cut the huge stone sections out of the earth—stone that was shipped off to build bridges and breakwalls.

It was 1902 when Brice decided to become a mortician. This left him with lots of spare time to work on his art on his farm. One after another, the statues began to accumulate, and they grew larger. He had a ready supply of sandstone.

He carved former Ohioan and President Warren G. Harding.

Some say he also did General George Custer, who hailed from nearby New Rumley.

By the 1920s, people had heard of Baughman's forest of sculptures and were asking to see them. By the 1940s, the park was a popular spot for visitors. People would come to stare at the statues of President James Garfield and General James McPherson, or at an elephant's head, or an eagle in flight. But in 1954, when Baughman moved off the farm and into town, the park was sold. The land went through several owners, who, for the most part, left the statuary alone to take on a patina of moss and climbing weeds. The last owner had hoped to turn it into a campground, but failing health prompted the sale to the Long-aberger Company that was developing the valley below. Baughman Park is not open to the public.

World's Largest Collection of Popcorn Poppers and Peanut Roasters

MARION

Also at Heritage Hall is the world's largest collection of antique popcorn poppers and peanut roasters, at the **Wyandot Popcorn Museum** (169 E. Church St., Marion; 740-387-4255). Worried that your favorite model might not be included? Don't be. Museum literature assures us that "all of the classic antique poppers are here—Dunbar, Kingery, Holcome and Hoke, Stutsman, Long-Eakin, Excel, Manley, Burch, Star, Bartholomew, Olsen, and Advance"—even "the original 1890 Patent Olsen Squirrel Cage Dry Popper"(!) For those who like a little celebrity flavor, there's the 1908 Dunbar Concession Wagon used by Paul Newman to promote his gourmet popcorn.

Popcorn diehards congregate at the annual Marion Popcorn Festival in downtown Marion (which claims to be "The World's Popcorn Capital") on the Thursday, Friday, and Saturday after Labor Day.

The Floating Island

MILLERSPORT

There's an unusual island in central Ohio. Most islands tend to stay put, but this island floats.

Believed to be the only one of its kind in the world, **Cranberry Bog** floats in the middle of Buckeye Lake State Park (740-467-2690) near Columbus.

A great glacier covered Ohio thousands of years ago, and it created shallow lakes and swamps as it retreated north. The area that was to become Buckeye Lake was one of these, and on the edge of the lake was a swampy area mostly made up of a cranberry-sphagnum moss bog.

In 1826, with the advent of Ohio's canal system and the need for "feeder" lakes to supply water to the canal, canal builders impounded the shallow, swampy lake, diverting streams and creeks into it to create Buckeye Lake. As the water started to rise, the cranberry-sphagnum bog broke loose from the bottom and began to float. It still floats today.

The island is mostly made up of sphagnum moss, with a large number of cranberries and pitcher plants, creating a spongelike meadow. A boardwalk allows visitors to cross the floating island, which is now a state nature preserve and National Natural Landmark. It can only be reached by boat, and visitors must have a permit from the Ohio Department of Natural Resources.

ODNR experts are concerned for the future of the floating island, because as birds deposit tree seeds on the shoreline and trees begin to grow, their weight and root spread tears large sections of the island loose; the land mass is shrinking rapidly.

Jim McCormack of the ODNR Natural Areas and Preserves said that from an area of nearly 50 acres 150 years ago, the island has now shrunk to less than 11 acres, and despite their efforts to stop the erosion, it may disappear in another half century.

Dixie and Other Songs

MOUNT VERNON

The song of the south was written by an Ohioan.

Daniel Decatur Emmett was born and died in Mount Vernon. He wrote a lot of music in his life, including "The Blue-tail Fly" ("Jimmy cracked corn and I don't care . . .") and "Turkey in the Straw." But he's best known for a song he wrote in 1859—"Dixie" ("I wish I was in the land of cotton . . ."). An instant hit, it was being sung in the North as well as the South when the Civil War started. But during the war, the song became the unofficial battle song of the South—much to the dismay of Emmett, who was not a Southern sympathizer.

Eventually, the song became popular again in the North, thanks to Abe Lincoln. On the night the Civil War ended, a crowd had gathered at the White House and was clamoring for a speech by the president. Lincoln came to the window, said a few words, then noticed a band in the crowd. He asked the band to play "Dixie," saying, "I've always liked the tune, and it belongs to all of us now."

Emmett is buried in **Mound View Cemetery** (307 Wooster Rd., Mt. Vernon). A memorial tribute to him donated by the Ohio division of the Daughters of the Confederacy is at the **Knox County Historical Society Museum** (875 Harcourt Rd., Mt. Vernon; 740-393-5247) A stone and plaque on South Mulbury Street mark the spot where his birthplace once stood (the house, now located off South Main Street, is open for tours by appointment with the historical society).

World's Largest Gourd Show
MT. GILEAD

EVENTS!

The **Ohio Gourd Show** bills itself as *the* place to learn about gourds.

And what might you learn about gourds? Well, they're flowering plants of the order *Cucurbitales*, for starters. The most common ones are cucumbers, watermelons, pumpkins, and squash. Some gourds are eaten; some are dried and used as containers or musical instruments. Some, apparently, just look great hanging around the house.

This show is no Johnny-come-lately; it's been held since 1962, always on the first full weekend in October. It features several buildings of gourd exhibits, gourd craft demonstrations, gourd lectures in a Gourd Theater, plenty of down-home gourd music, and . . . a hog roast.

Oh, and if you have too much hog at the roast, look for some cucurbitacin—the bitter substance found in gourds. It's used as a purgative.

THE ONLY STATE
WITHOUT A FLAG

Ohio is the only state without a flag. Ohio's "flag" is, technically, not a flag but a burgee. A burgee is a sort of twin-tailed pennant. Ohio is the only state that uses one.

It was designed by John Eisemann, a state official. The large blue triangle represents Ohio's hills and valleys, while the white and red stripes are said to represent roads and waterways. The stars, 13 of them, in the blue field represent the original 13 colonies of the United States. Four stars at the peak of the blue field are for the states added after the initial 13 and point to Ohio as the 17th state admitted to the Union. It is claimed that the large red circle surrounded by a white "O" stands for "Ohio."

Historian Richard McElroy points out that the burgee was first flown at the Ohio building at the Pan-American Exposition in 1901 and closely resembles a banner carried by explorer Christopher Columbus on his expedition to the New World in 1492. Since our state capital was named for Columbus, it's possible that the explorer also influenced the design of the Ohio flag, which was adopted by the legislature in 1902.

World's Biggest Basket

NEWARK

When the boss says he wants a building that looks like a basket, that's what he gets—at least at the **Longaberger Company** (One Market Square, 1500 E. Main St., Newark; 740-322-5588).

The late Dave Longaberger, when CEO of the basket firm, wanted a new corporate office building. He, company officials, and architects met for long hours trying to decide what it should look like but were unable to agree on a plan. Dave excused himself from the meeting and left the room. A few minutes later he returned carrying the company's trademark "Market Basket."

As he set the basket on the table he said, "This is what this company is all about. This is what our office is going to look like."

Sure, there were a few obvious objections from his committee. And probably a few people who said it couldn't be done. But in the end he got what he asked for: an exact replica of the Medium Market Basket—only 160 times larger.

When the boss says he wants a basket-shaped world headquarters, who's going to argue? No one at the Longaberger Company.

Today it is the centerpiece of a 25-acre corporate campus. At least 500 people work inside the seven-story building, which covers 180,000 square feet.

The basket handles, which weigh almost 150 tons, had to be set in place using giant cranes. They feature a humidity sensor that turns on heat to keep ice from forming on them. There are 84 windows in the building.

What made construction especially difficult was the basket's shape: it is smaller at the base than at the top. It is 192 feet long and 126 feet wide at ground level, but at the seventh-floor level it expands to 208 feet by 142 feet. Inside is a seven-story, 30,000-square-foot atrium. The building's offices are arranged around the atrium. There is also a 142-seat auditorium in the structure.

Visitors are welcome to stop in and look around. The company asks that large groups call ahead for a reservation.

Largest Living Sign

NEWARK

The **Dawes Arboretum** (7770 Jacksontown Rd. SE, Newark; 740-323-2355) in Newark boasts what may be the largest living signboard in Ohio, if not the country. The sign, which reads "DAWES ARBORE-TUM," is actually a series of shrubs 2,040 feet long. It can best be seen from a nearby observation tower.

World's Largest Crystal Ball

WESTERVILLE

What is the world's largest crystal ball doing in a ceramic society headquarters? It belongs there, actually, because glass is technically a ceramic.

Why make the world's largest crystal ball? Now, that's a better question, perhaps best answered by the age-old rhetorical retort, Why not? The world's largest crystal ball is, at 573 millimeters in diameter, not so big compared to other "world's largest" items, but it is pretty darned heavy—700 pounds.

The ball is on display at the **American Ceramic Society Headquarters** (600 N. Cleveland Ave., Westerville; 866-721-3322). Admission is free. Aren't ceramics wonderful?

NORTHWEST
OHIO

Oldest Concrete Road in America

Concrete pavement usually lasts 20 to 30 years without needing major repairs, while asphalt usually holds up for only 8 to 12 years before needing resurfacing.

Think about this the next time you are sitting in a long line on an interstate highway lined with orange barrels, watching a construction crew adding new layers of asphalt to the highway. I would swear that I sometimes see the same workers year after year working on the same stretch of highway.

The city fathers of Bellefontaine must have considered these facts over a hundred years ago when they voted to pave the streets around the Logan County Courthouse. The person in charge was a man by the name of George Bartholomew, the creator of Portland concrete. What better place to demonstrate the value of concrete than the streets of his hometown? He must have done a good job. The year was 1891, and this was the **first concrete highway in America**; over a century later, the street is still in use.

Incidentally, one of the streets around the courthouse is named McKinley Street in honor of the president, who came from Ohio. It is said to be the shortest street in the world.

Highest Point in Ohio

BELLEFONTAINE

The highest point in Ohio is not a rocky crag . . . or even much of a hill. It's a vocational school. On a gentle slope about 2 miles outside of Bellefontaine, the **Ohio Hi-Point Career Center** (2280 State Rte. 540, Bellefontaine) rises above all else in the state at an elevation of

1,549 feet. (It's closed evenings and weekends, so if you want to reach the summit of the state, go during school hours: 7 a.m. to 7 p.m., Monday through Friday.) Thanks to Campbell Hill, as the rise is known, Bellefontaine stakes its claim as "The Top of Ohio."

World's Largest Collection of Postmarks

BELLEVUE

The world's largest collection of postmark history—more than a million items—is located in two small historical buildings in Bellevue.

The museum was the dream of Margie Pfund of Columbiana, who started collecting postmarks and postmark-related items in one room of her house in the 1940s. She started getting lots of donations and had to move the museum several times. It eventually landed in two buildings that are part of **Historic Lyme Village** (open in summer or by appointment; 5001 State Rte. 4, Bellevue; 419-483-4949).

Postmarks rule here, of course (the museum is run by members of the Postmark Collectors Club). They are collected here in huge numbers—mostly mounted in binders and covered with protective Mylar. The museum also houses more than 1,500 publications related to postal history and a few vintage post-office boxes and canceling stamps.

The Three Fingers of Mary Bach and Clark Gable's Pheasant

BOWLING GREEN

Three human fingers in a jar have made the Wood County Historical Center famous. I'm sure they would rather be known for the many other, normal, wonderful historical exhibits they also have on display, but it's the fingers in a jar that most schoolkids want to see when they come to visit.

THE RICE BOWL OF OHIO

ARCHBOLD

You probably don't realize it, but America's favorite Asian food is made in Ohio.

La Choy Foods is located in the middle of rural Archbold, tucked away in the northwest corner of the Buckeye State.

Two friends from the University of Michigan formed the La Choy Asian Food Company in Detroit back in 1920. Wally Smith had a grocery store and wanted to offer his customers freshly grown bean sprouts. He turned to his college friend, Ilhan New, who was born in Korea, to learn how to grow them.

They started a sprout garden in Smith's bathtub. (He must have used it himself only one night a week, because the sprouts take about six days to mature.)

What brought them to Archbold? Location and handy ingredients. Northwest Ohio has lots of cows and chickens. Nearby Michigan grows a lot of celery. It's just a short drive to Pennsylvania, where they grow big mushrooms. The lake port and railroads in nearby Toledo make importation of other items pretty easy. And that's why Asian food is made in the heartland—Ohio. (Now they use large concrete vats to raise the sprouts instead of bathtubs.)

The fingers belonged to Mary Bach of Bowling Green, who was savagely murdered by her husband, Carl, in October of 1881. They had not had a happy marriage, and on that day something drove Carl to get a large machete from the barn and to kill his wife and then hack her up, cutting off bits and pieces of her body, including the three fingers, which were exhibited, pickled in a jar, during his trial.

Carl was convicted of Mary's murder, and he had the distinction of being the last man in Wood County to be hanged publicly on the courthouse steps. In fact, the county sold tickets to his execution, which was held on the final day of the county fair. They really knew how to get a crowd to the county fair in those days! In fact, the tickets were in such demand that scalpers got into the act and sold tickets for much above the stated price.

The historical center also has on display the noose used in the hanging, the corn knife that Carl used to chop up his wife, and one of the tickets for admission to the hanging.

The grisly display was exhibited for many years in the Wood County courthouse, along with some other items from famous local trials, to demonstrate that crime does not pay.

It's the three pickled fingers in a jar that most schoolkids want to see when they come to the museum.

When the Wood County Home was converted into a historical museum, the grim exhibit was transferred there.

The **Wood County Historical Center** (13660 County Home Rd., Bowling Green; 419-352-0967) offers a real frozen-in-time look at nineteenth-century rural America, from a replica of a small general store to a collection of early oil-drilling rigs. They even have a pheasant that movie star Clark Gable shot while hunting in Wood County in the 1930s.

Remember the Maine and Pass the Soap

FINDLAY

At the close of almost every war this country gets into, patriotic citizens want a souvenir to put in their park or in front of the town hall. Most always, these take the shape of old field guns, or sometimes a surplus tank or even an airplane (depending on the clout of the local congressional delegation).

Well, the rush was on after the 1898 Spanish-American War, when it became known that the greatest symbol of that conflict, the battleship *USS Maine*, was being raised from the floor of Havana harbor. (It was the mysterious explosion of the *Maine* and the loss of American lives on board that triggered the war.) Just about every community started making a pitch for a part of the old ship.

Considering that the man who had ordered the *Maine* to Cuba, President William McKinley, was an Ohioan, Ohio towns figured they'd have an edge on the competition when it came to relics.

And they did. The base of the conning tower, the command center of the *Maine*, was sent to McKinley's home town of Canton. Other parts of the ship were made into plaques and given to Berea and Elyria.

But the real catch was made by the town of Findlay. They got the ship captain Charles Sigsbee's bathtub.

Congressman Frank Willis, from Urbana, used his influence to ask for something no one else had thought of, the captain's tub. He got it intending to donate it to his own home town. Local folks,

however, didn't see anything terribly heroic about a bathtub. They asked instead for a 10-inch shell from one of the ship's big guns.

While Urbana was saying "no thanks," the city of Boston, Massachusetts, got into the act, insisting that the tub belonged there, because that was where the ship's captain had hailed from. While the controversy swirled, the city of Findlay was heard from. They offered to take the bathtub, and because Findlay was in Congressman Willis's district, next door to Urbana, that seemed like a convenient solution. Except the navy had already delivered the bathtub to Urbana, and the mayor of Urbana was storing it in his chicken house. He refused to give it up to Findlay unless he got the 10-inch shell. Willis finally settled the matter by talking the navy into sending the shell to Urbana, in exchange for which Urbana sent the bathtub to Findlay—allegedly C.O.D., though the town of Findlay never got around to paying.

And that was but the start of the odyssey in store for the bathtub of the *USS Maine*.

On March 3, 1913, the bathtub finally reached Findlay. Then the citizens discovered they had made a lot of fuss over a galvanized tub that had been underwater for 14 years—and it just wasn't much to look at. Interest in the relic waned rapidly, and the tub was stored in the local municipal building. Its celebrity declined further, and the tub eventually ended up being used to store coal for the city building.

Ultimately the news broke that Findlay was using the bathtub as a coal bin, and the neighboring town of Lima jumped into the fray. They demanded the tub. But Findlay's Spanish-American War veterans came to the rescue first, hauling the tub out of the municipal building and promising to bronze it and put it in a park someplace in town. They may have had good intentions, but they wound up just putting the tub into a display case in a back hall of the Hancock County Courthouse in Findlay. It moved around the courthouse for the next 45 years, like an old soldier just fading away.

In 1960 the courthouse was renovated, and the tub was given to the Findlay College Museum. They decided the display case was more important and used that instead, putting the bathtub into storage. Then, in 1974, Findlay College was cleaning house and ended up giving the tub to the **Hancock Historical Museum** (422 W. Sandusky St., Findlay; 419-423-4433)—for *their* basement.

But the bathtub has once again been resurrected. New management at the museum has brought it out for display. It's no prettier than it was in 1913, in fact even more of the enamel is missing, and it's rusty, but it *is* a bathtub from a ship that helped start a war.

And name another town that has a bathtub for a war memorial.

A Disputed Presidential Election

FREMONT

Quick. Which president of the United States was involved in a disputed election in which the vote count in Florida was crucial, and after which he had a long wait to find out if he had won?

If you answered George W. Bush, you are only half right. The first time this happened, it was to an Ohioan, Rutherford B. Hayes.

In fact, his election finally had to be settled by Congress. You can learn all about this and a whole lot of other interesting things at the **Rutherford B. Hayes Presidential** Center (Spiegel Grove, Fremont; 800-998-7737). As it happens, this was also the very first presidential library and museum in the country. The former president's estate contains not only his library and museum, but also the home where he died and his grave.

Did you know that Hayes was the only Ohio president to die in Ohio? And that Lucy Webb Hayes, the president's wife, was the very first presidential wife to be called the First Lady? That Hayes, a Civil War veteran, was wounded four times in battle?

By the way, close to President Hayes's own grave is the final resting place of Old Whitey—the president's beloved war horse, who survived 19 battles.

Old Whitey's war record earned him a burial plot next to the president's.

The Gates of the White House in Ohio

FREMONT

They didn't pick them up at a garage sale, but it was something like that that brought the fancy ornamental iron gates that once guarded the White House in Washington, D.C., to Fremont, Ohio.

The heavy steel gates, bearing various ornamental seals, were first erected around the White House in 1871 to control horse-and-buggy traffic entering West Executive Avenue from Pennsylvania Avenue.

By the time World War I rolled around, the narrow gateways, perfect for horses and carriages, were just too small for the growing numbers of motorcars now using the streets around the White House.

In 1921 Colonel Webb C. Hayes, eldest son of former president Rutherford B. Hayes, was in Washington shopping for appropriate gates for his father's former estate in Fremont, which he had opened to the public as the country's first presidential library. Someone told Hayes about the ornamental gates around the White House, which had by now become a real traffic hazard.

Webb Hayes, who held the nation's highest award for bravery, the Medal of Honor, called on the current president, Warren G. Harding, another Ohioan, and suggested that if the White House had no further need for the gates, he would be happy to give them a good home in Ohio. Harding was delighted with the idea, but when congressmen heard about the deal they said, "Wait a minute." The gates belonged to the country, and it was up to Congress to decide how they were to be disposed of.

Despite Harding's backing, it took Hayes six years of persistence and legal wrangling with bureaucrats and Congress to finally have the gates, which were no longer in use, transferred to the Fremont estate.

The ornamental gates that guarded the White House during the stay of every president from Ulysses Grant to Calvin Coolidge, can now be seen at the six entrances to the **Rutherford B. Hayes Presidential Center** (Spiegel Grove, Fremont; 800-998-7737) thanks to the persistence of Colonel Webb C. Hayes, who refused to take "no" for an answer.

The Historic Privy of Genoa

GENOA

Picture this. It's the nation's bicentennial, and your little community is feeling a bit left out. Towns and villages all over America are sprucing up old buildings and putting them on the National Register of Historic Places to do their part for America's big birthday celebration.

But the oldest building you've got is . . . a bit unusual.

That's what happened in Genoa. Their oldest building, which had been built around the time of the Civil War, was a small brick structure out behind a local school. It definitely showed its age, but contractors said that with some repairs—expensive repairs—it would probably look as good as new.

The problem was, their building had originally

YOU SAY LEE-MA,
I SAY LIME-AH

**Ohio shares a lot of place names with more
famous cities throughout the world. But that doesn't
mean we have to pronounce them the same way.**

In Peru, Lima is pronounced "Lee-ma." In Ohio, it's "Lime-ah".
There is "Med-eena," Spain and "Med-eye-na," Ohio.
"Mee-lon" is in Italy; "My-lun" is in Ohio.
Most Daltons say it like it looks, but in Ohio it's "Daal-ton."
In Germany it's "Bur-LIN." In most of Ohio we say, "BUR-lin."
Cadiz, Ohio, is pronounced "Cadis," but the one in Spain is
"Kah-DIZ."

In the old world, Athens was pronounced "Ath-ens," but in
Ohio there is New "Ay-thens"

By the way, how do you pronounce a town name that only has
two letters? Ai, Ohio, would, I guess, be pronounced "A" or "I." For
the record, Ai is located in northwest Ohio, in Fulton County.

Mantua trips up news broadcasters in Ohio all the time. It
looks like "Man-too-a," but it's pronounced "Mant-a-way."

Folks in "Lo-dye" love it when you don't say "Load-ee" for Lodi.

In Hamilton the local folks got so excited about their town
they added an exclamation mark after the name to make sure
that everyone knew they were talking about Hamilton! Ohio.

served the teachers and the students of the local school as their "little house." The building was a 12-hole brick privy.

Genoa keeps current, of course, and the school had long ago stopped using the privy for its original purpose. It had survived,

probably, because of its size, and the fact that it was, well, built like a brick privy! So the holes had been filled in and the seats taken out, and it became a storage building for the school janitor. Down through the years, many people had even forgotten what the little building's original purpose was.

But locals weren't shy when it came to saving their decrepit old toilet building, and they convinced their congressman that the building was indeed worth renovating. He managed to get a grant through Congress, and once the paperwork was done, Genoa, Ohio, became the only community in America with an outhouse listed on the National Register of Historic Places.

A Real Pigskin Festival
HARROD

EVENTS!

Take a hunk of skin off a pig, burn the hair off of it, then toss the skin into a deep fryer until it puffs up all golden brown. Then you pop it in your mouth. Yum.

What you might call a real pigskin festival is held each year in the town of Harrod, near Lima. Pork rinds are the polite name for what I described above, and they are a snack food loved by millions of people, including former U.S. president George H. W. Bush, who confessed he preferred pork rinds to broccoli.

You can cook pigskin, or pork rinds, by deep-frying, microwaving, or boiling. They are also used as fish food. You can learn more fascinating facts each year in Harrod at the two-day **Pork Rind Heritage Festival** (Main Street, Harrod; 419-648-5091).

Hard to Swallow

LIMA

Estey Yingling started the collection. His son, Walter "Bud" Yingling, continued it and ultimately donated it to the **Allen County Museum** (620 W. Market St., Lima; 419-222-9426). Father and son, both physicians (ear, nose, and throat specialists), collected objects swallowed by local residents (including patients at nearby Lima Mental Hospital). "I've never actually counted them," said John Carnes, curator of this, the largest county museum in Ohio, "but there's well over a hundred." Asked what might be the prize of the collection, Carnes said, "There's a very large wood screw that kind of stands out."

The museum collection also boasts a John Dillinger exhibit (he broke out of the local jail in 1933 and killed a sheriff), a restored Sherman tank, a large collection of albino animals (stuffed), and a children's museum.

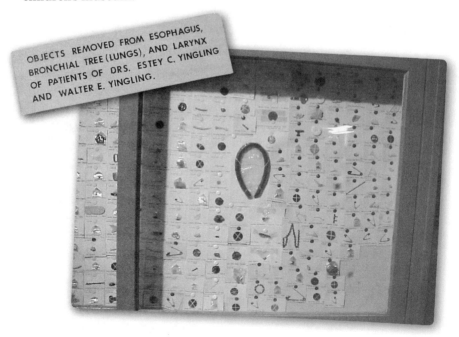

OBJECTS REMOVED FROM ESOPHAGUS, BRONCHIAL TREE (LUNGS), AND LARYNX OF PATIENTS OF DRS. ESTEY C. YINGLING AND WALTER E. YINGLING.

Mystery Hill

MARBLEHEAD

"Visit Mystery Hill and defy the laws of nature and gravity," the sign says. Well, that's hard to resist. And besides, it comes complete with dinosaurs. **Mystery Hill** (8232 E. Harbor Rd., Marblehead; 419-798-5230) fits right in here in Ohio's "vacationland."

Our guide, who appeared to be 10 or 11 years old, warned us that "horses have been known to stampede and small children become hysterical" upon seeing what we were about to experience.

Inside the rather tumble-down building, our "guide" put a golf ball in a trough and it ran uphill. He then pumped a pump, and the water ran uphill. Sensing he was not impressing his audience, the lad cheerfully announced, that he would overcome gravity in a "death-defying act," and with that he placed the back legs of a kitchen chair on a two-by-four nailed to the wall, hopped on the seat, and seemingly hung in space supported only by the two back legs.

The tilted floor made all of us feel as though we were walking at a 45 degree tilt.

Our young guide informed us that the hillside location was chosen for this attraction because of its "massive gravitational pull from the center of the earth."

You can't miss Mystery Hill's sister attraction, Prehistoric Forest—a 15-foot-tall fiberglass dinosaur stands guard in front of a fake mountain that belches fluorescent colored flames and features a manmade waterfall. That'll get you in the mood for a stroll through the forest.

There are 19 life-size beasts, including a triceratops and a *T. rex*. Some are displayed in wooded glades, others in marshy ponds. A couple of them make some noise and have mechanical heads that wig and wag, but if you're looking for animatronic dinosaurs this is not the place to find them. Here they pretty much just stand and stare at you. All in all, even the smallest child will probably not be frightened by an afternoon walk through here.

"Horses have been known to stampede and small children become hysterical," warned our young guide.

The Marblehead Muffler Man

MARBLEHEAD

"Muffler Man" is a designation given to huge fiberglass statues of men or women, usually cradling a product in their arms, often along major highways, and near especially publicity-minded businesses. Originally some of them were used to promote muffler shops; hence the name. One such Muffler Man has stood on the Marblehead Peninsula for over a quarter of a century, but most folks can't remember what he was selling or how he got there. He stands, 20 feet tall but empty handed now, in front of a camper-trailer business. Most locals say it's been years since they have seen **Big Pierre**, as they call him, sell anything. Standing guard along State Route 163, east of SR 269, Pierre laughs at the rain and the snow. In fact nothing seems to bother him except the passing of time.

But Big Pierre is really Big Jacques. He started life in Mansfield as the representative of Jacques' Roast Beef Sandwiches. His arms, which once reportedly held a sandwich or a pizza box, are just skeletal frames now. His white sailor hat is dirty and disfigured. His present owner, Young's Travel Trailers, says he is for sale.

A Very Happy Walleye to You
PORT CLINTON

EVENTS!

On New Year's Eve in Times Square, a crystal glass apple is lowered down a tower to announce the transition from one year to the next. That's because New York is popularly known as the Big Apple.

Well, little Port Clinton, Ohio, decided to get in on the act. And what would you expect to find in the port whose 1,000 chartered fishermen take in about 70 percent of Lake Erie's walleye catch each year? That's right: a 20-foot-long fiberglass walleye named Captain Wylie.

Can it be long until the New Year's Eve when TV cameras will switch instead to the frosty shores of Lake Erie to watch Captain Wylie drop in Port Clinton?

Captain Wylie, a 20-foot-long walleye, appears ready to swallow a 4-foot-tall child.

Big Fruit

PORT CLINTON

Of course, if Port Clinton wants to compete with the Big Apple, they can also compete with their . . . big apple. A five-foot-tall Red Delicious stands out along the roadside at **Bergman's Fruit Farm** (Catawba Rd., just north of the U.S. Rte. 2 interchange).

The Ship on the Island

PUT-IN-BAY

On the ferry ride back from South Bass Island to Port Clinton, a lot of people grab for the camera and a few stare in disbelief upon seeing a Great Lakes ore boat stuck into a cliff, hundreds of feet above the water. It looks for all the world as if a giant storm had deposited the ship, bow forward, on this cliff overlooking the lake.

Don't bother to look through the tourist books for it. There are no brochures, no maps pointing it out, and no explanations of how it got there.

The story behind the ship is becoming a Lake Erie legend, though.

The ship began life nearly 80 years ago as the *Benson Ford* flagship of the Ford Motor Company's fleet of lake freighters. Henry Ford named it after one of his grandsons. He took a special interest in the ship and had luxury accommodations put into its forward section: walnut-paneled staterooms, a fireplace in a gathering room, a special kitchen, special plumbing. It was a ship that was to be fit for a king, or at least the founder of an auto dynasty. Whether Henry Ford ever actually sailed on the *Benson Ford* is a matter of conjecture, but certainly many of the top Ford executives and their families made use of the luxury quarters over the half-century that it sailed the Great Lakes. It was retired from service and scheduled to be cut up for scrap in 1986.

At that time, Frank and Lydia Sullivan were looking for a summer home on the Lake Erie Islands. Finding nothing they liked, they were considering building one when Frank heard that the *Benson Ford* was being scrapped. Discovering that the owner's quarters had been constructed for Henry Ford, he realized that it would be very special. That's when a dream was born: to cut off the front of the *Benson Ford*, from the owner's quarters all the way up to the pilothouse, and move it to South Bass Island for a home.

After thousands and thousands of dollars, and hours and hours of frustration, finally the front section was cut away and loaded onto a huge barge that then towed the *Benson Ford* (now renamed, of course, the **Frank Sullivan**) 60 miles west from Cleveland to the Lake Erie Islands.

Frank and Lydia purchased a landlocked lot on a small hill overlooking the water on the western edge of South Bass Island. Both sea-borne and land-based cranes made the final transfer of the *Frank Sullivan* from the barge

onto a solid bedrock foundation, the bow nearly hanging over the 18-foot cliff above the water. And the *Benson Ford/Frank Sullivan* was home from the seas.

After spending thousands of more dollars in heat, electrical, and plumbing hookups, the Sullivans were ready to tackle the renovation of the quarters in their boat home.

Over the next 13 years, the *Frank Sullivan* was the summer home they had planned. At one point they even considered turning the landmark into a bed-and-breakfast to help offset some of the enormous costs they had incurred moving the ship to the islands. However, because their lot was landlocked, their neighbors were required by law only to allow the Sullivans access to their home, not to tolerate commercial traffic.

That effectively stopped any commercial use of the unusual home. And when the Sullivans decided to finally sell the ship home in 1999, there was a new problem. How do you price something unique? There was nothing even remotely similar to it anywhere. So they finally put the place up for public auction. They advertised it for weeks and drew inquiries from 10 states and Canada. The big day finally arrived on September 21, 1999. The ship residence was sold for $451,000 to two local automobile dealers. There had been speculation that the unusual residence would bring as much as a million or more dollars.

The *Frank Sullivan* can be seen by arriving and departing ferryboat passengers on the western side of South Bass Island. It is still a private home and is not open to the public.

The Longest Bar in the World

PUT-IN-BAY

If it pleases you to see a bartender sling a couple of cold brews down a wet bar, you have to see the bar at the **Beer Barrel Saloon** (324 Delaware St., Put-in-Bay; 419-285-2337) on South Bass Island in Lake Erie.

Their bar is the longest in the world, according to the *Guinness Book of World Records*. To put it in perspective, if you stood the bar on end it would be taller than the island's other main tourist attraction, the Perry's Victory and International Peace Memorial. It's 405 feet, 10 inches long. It has 160 bar stools, and 56 beer taps, and on a busy night more than 20 bartenders work behind it.

Rudolph the Ohio Reindeer

RUDOLPH

Rudolph, Ohio, is little more than a wide spot in the highway in northwest Ohio. The population in and around the little town is probably less than a thousand. But when the Christmas season arrives, hundreds of thousands of letters pour into the little town's post office.

Marsha Deitemyer is the officer in charge of the **Rudolph post office** (Rudolph Postmaster, P.O. Box 9998, Rudolph). She says last Christmas she and her husband and two kids worked almost every night to hand-cancel more than 130,000 pieces of mail that had

been sent to Rudolph to be remailed with the Rudolph postmark.

The postmark is applied with a rubber stamp marked "Reindeer Station," with a small picture of the reindeer with a glowing nose.

Marsha says the mail comes from all over America, and that the post office has been providing the holiday service for several years.

Don't forget, if you send your boxed cards to Marsha to remail and cancel, you have to have proper postage on each envelope. It's the holidays and Marsha has the holiday spirit, but she's not going to pay for your postage.

World's Largest Motorcycle T-shirt

SANDUSKY

T-shirts with advertising on them have become an American icon. People the world over wear them, advertising everything imaginable—and some things that are unimaginable. Some people love their T-shirts so much that when the shirts finally wear out they have parts of them woven into quilts to sleep with at night.

T-shirts are made in every size, from tiny-tees that fit newborn babies all the way up to extra-large T-shirts that will fit even the most rotund human being. The good folks at **Roeder Harley-Davidson Motorcycles** (5316 Milan Rd./State Rte. 250), Sandusky; 419-621-1046) in Sandusky display what they claim is the world's largest motorcycle T-shirt. It's 11 feet by 11 feet. To put it another way, it's 50 times larger than the biggest human T-shirt. Made for the Ohio store by a Dallas, Texas, company, the shirt has 121 square feet of 100-percent cotton jersey. That's bigger than some living room rugs. The finished shirt weighs more than 15 pounds. It hangs in a Harley-Davidson store that is a replica of the original Harley plant in Milwaukee, Wisconsin.

A Place Where They Write on Your Buns

TOLEDO

Tony Packo's would probably be just another neighborhood bar in Toledo had it not been for some very famous customers. One was a skinny kid who grew up nearby and went on to become a TV star. Jamie Farr played Corporal Max Klinger on the hit TV show *M*A*S*H*, and in many of the shows he made mention of his longing for a Hungarian hot dog from Tony Packo's. The real-life Tony Packo's benefited greatly from the national and worldwide exposure. Jamie Farr, they say, has free hot dogs at Tony Packo's for life.

But an earlier brush with fame, in 1972, also had an impact on the business. Movie star Burt Reynolds was performing in *The Rainmaker* at a Toledo-area theater, and Nancy Packo, Tony's daughter, wrote him a note and suggested that since he had to eat somewhere, he should try their place.

Two nights later, much to everyone's surprise, Reynolds and other cast members walked in. The Packo family wanted Reynolds to sign his autograph on something that they could put on the wall. They searched for a blank piece of paper, but none could readily be found, so in their haste to mark the night, someone grabbed a stale hot-dog bun and offered that to Reynolds to sign.

Now, local and national celebrities get asked to sign the darndest things—everything from ladies' underwear to a bare chest. So the fact he was signing his autograph on a hot-dog bun probably didn't even phase Reynolds. But in that moment a tradition was born.

Today there are more than a thousand autographed hot-dog buns mounted throughout the restaurant. They bear the signatures of five U.S. presidents, as well as first ladies, sports figures, local celebrities (like traveling reporters!), and, of course, Burt Reynolds, the man who started it all.

Tony Packo II, who took over the restaurant from his father, says to his knowledge it's the only collection of autographed hot-dog buns in the world.

But here's a secret: they aren't real. Tony says that the very first ones were, but they started to turn green and disintegrate pretty quickly, so they sent a mold of a bun to a factory and had some styrofoam buns made. Unless you bite into one, you can't tell the difference.

The Packos now operate a chain of restaurants in northwest Ohio, but the original **Tony Packo's** (1902 Front St., Toledo; 419-691-6054), where Corporal Klinger first enjoyed a Hungarian hot dog, is still at the same location.

Nice buns, Leslie Uggams. You too, Mel Tormé!

In their haste to mark the night,
someone grabbed a stale hot-dog bun
and offered that to Burt Reynolds.

NORTHEAST OHIO

A Hotel with Round Rooms

You'll never be "cornered" in a round room. You can make that observation when you stay at **Quaker Square Inn at the University of Akron** (135 S. Broadway, Akron; 330-253-5970).

The rooms really are round. And almost totally soundproof. They were carved out of a cluster of 36 concrete silos once used by the Quaker Oats Company to store the grain that they used to make such things as Quaker Oats. (Remember "The cereal shot from guns"?) The complex, which had been built around the turn of the twentieth century, was finally abandoned when the parent company moved to Chicago, and the city fathers in Akron started looking around for a new use for the site, which is very near downtown Akron.

The answer was an innovative idea to turn the old mill into a shopping center and the silos into a hotel. Work started in 1973, and the hotel opened about two years later.

The silos, listed on the National Register of Historic Places, are each 120 feet tall and 24 feet in diameter. The hotel can claim to be the only one in the world where all the rooms are round.

The Akron Airdock

AKRON

It sits at the edge of an airfield. In the twilight you might think it was the body of some giant prehistoric animal, all dark gray and black, merging with the night.

The **Airdock in Akron** was built in 1929 by the Goodyear Tire & Rubber Company to construct and house giant rigid airships, which were three or four times longer than today's blimps.

How big is it? It's equal in height to a 22-story building, and you could play seven football games side by side on the floor inside. It is twice the length of the Washington Monument. When it was built, it boasted the largest continuous area ever contained under one roof.

Each of the spherical doors weighs 600 tons and is fastened at the top with a steel pin 17 inches in diameter and six feet long.

This is a place of legend. The hollow building has been known to develop its own weather. Clouds form, and light rain has even fallen inside. Outside, after a heavy snow, they once experienced an avalanche of snow off the rounded roof that was so heavy a nearby security office at the base of the building was flattened.

No tours are allowed in the building, but the exterior of the Airdock can be seen from just about anywhere near the airport or from Kelley Avenue, near the Carousel Dinner Theater.

Dinosaurs on Noah's Ark?

AKRON

Did Noah have a *T. rex* boarded next to a flock of lambs? Were pterodactyls sharing the perches with parrots?

An Akron, Ohio, museum claims that dinosaurs and other prehistoric animals were passengers on Noah's ark.

The creation-science-based museum, called the **Akron Fossil and Science Center** (2080 S. Cleveland-Massillon Rd., Copley; 330-665-3466), maintains it is possible that the theory of evolution taught by many scientists and researchers is wrong about how long ago dinosaurs roamed the earth. They offer a different interpretation of history, backed up partly by carvings found in Incan ruins in South America that show what appear to be men and dinosaurs fighting.

They even have a scale model of Noah's ark that includes several kinds of dinosaurs among the many common animals believed to have been on board.

In back of the museum is a large, dinosaur-themed playground for youngsters that includes a zip-line, a suspension bridge, and a place to launch paper airplanes.

You Can't Get There From Main Street

ALLIANCE

A lot of almanacs and trivia books have had fun over the years at the expense of the good people of Alliance, Ohio.

Okay. Yes. It's true. Main Street in downtown Alliance starts at a dead-end street and goes, guess where? To another dead-end street—giving Alliance the questionable honor of being perhaps the only town in America whose main street doesn't go anywhere.

Usually the main street in a community is a continuation of a main highway that connects the town with other communities.

But no one ever offers an explanation of why this strange situation happened in Alliance.

Margaret Albright of the reference department at the **Rodman Public Library** (215 E. Broadway St., Alliance; 330-821-2665) in Alliance has a ready answer when asked, though.

She admits it is a fact that Main Street dead-ends on Sawburg Avenue at one end of the street and Webb Avenue at the other end. You have to twist and turn several times to reach a main highway to drive out of town. However, she also points to the fact that Alliance was founded in a time when railroads were the principal means of transportation and that the city of Alliance was located at the junction of two railroad rights of way. Ms. Albright says, "From this railroad crossing, the first streets were laid out, extending west."

So Main Street, which was the "main" street in the town, followed the railroad tracks west until stopping at a point just short of where one railroad turns south. In recent years Main Street has been extended farther west through Alliance's industrial park.

So there you have it. Alliance founders were not playing a practical joke on future motorists. Main Street was put where it was for the convenience of people who rode the train, which at that time was the most convenient and direct way to get in and out of town.

Largest Sandstone Quarry in the World

AMHERST

Amherst Township has a mighty big hole.

It also has a large sign over its bandstand proclaiming "Amherst, Ohio, Sandstone Center of the World." The two items go together, of course; many homes and businesses are made partly or entirely from sandstone that came from the giant quarries just outside of town.

American Stone Cleveland Quarries (8705 Quarry Rd., Amherst; 800-248-0250) has been quarrying and fabricating sandstone here since 1868. The quarries cover a thousand acres and contain over 300 million cubic feet of stone. The quarry hole in Amherst known as Buckeye Number One is believed to be the largest sandstone quarry hole in the world. It can easily be seen from Quarry Road, which runs from South Amherst to Amherst. Sandstone from here was used to build the John Hancock Building in Boston, the Hockey Hall of Fame in Toronto, and Buffalo's city hall.

HANG OUT WITH FAMOUS (DEAD) FOLKS

Do you want to hang out with famous people? Try visiting any one of dozens of Ohio cemeteries. Lots of famous people called Ohio home at one time, or had a special attraction to the Buckeye State—so much so that they decided to spend eternity here.

For example, at the Greenlawn Cemetery in Columbus, you can hobnob with Samuel Prescott Bush. He is the paternal grandfather of former president George Bush, and great-grandfather of President George W. Bush. He's in section 56, southwest of the chapel.

Not far away in that same cemetery you'll find Captain Eddie Rickenbacker, the World War I hero known as the "Ace of Aces" for the number of German planes he shot down. He later founded Eastern Airlines, which is now just a memory in aviation history.

Rickenbacker is just around the corner from Roy Stanislaus. Who was he? Stanislaus was a sergeant in the cavalry on the day Custer was wiped out at Little Big Horn. Stanislaus won the Medal of Honor for bringing water to the wounded during the famous battle.

In Spring Grove Cemetery in Cincinnati, you can visit Salmon P. Chase, secretary of the treasury during the Lincoln administration and member of the Supreme Court. And Powell Crosley, Jr., who invented the refrigerator bearing his name. (He also invented a tiny car called the Crosley and owned the Cincinnati Reds.) Also buried here is Charles Fleischman, the yeast manufacturer, James Norris Gamble (as in Procter & . . .); William Cooper Procter (the other half); Jesse and Hannah

Grant, parents of president Ulysses Grant; famed New York Yankees manager Miller Huggins; Bernard Kroger, who started the Kroger grocery store empire; several members of the Mc-Cook family (see, "The Fighting Mc-Cooks"); and Alexander McGuffey of McGuffey Readers.

In Cleveland's Lake View Cemetery, you'll find songwriter and singer Ernest Roland Ball (see, "When Irish Eyes Are Smiling") and Helene Hathaway Britton, who once owned the St. Louis Cardinals (the first woman to own a major league baseball club). There is a mass grave here honoring the 172 students and two teachers who died in America's biggest school fire, the Collinwood school fire, on March 4, 1908. Former Ohio governor Harry Davis is also buried here, as well as James Garfield, the assassinated twentieth U.S. president. (Technically, he and his wife, Lucretia Garfield, are not really buried here. Their bodies rest in a crypt beneath the monument that dominates this cemetery.) Also in Lake View Cemetery you'll find Coburn Haskell, the inventor of the modern golf ball; John Hay, private secretary to Abraham Lincoln and secretary of state to William McKinley; Dayton Clarence Miller, who produced the first X-ray of the human body; Gloria Pressman, one of the original "Little Rascals" of the movies; and the world's richest man, John D. Rockefeller, Sr. Have you ever tasted Salisbury steak? It was created by Dr. James Salisbury, who is also buried in Lake View Cemetery. Also buried here is Carl Stokes, the first African-American to be elected mayor of a major U.S. city.

Down in Dayton at Woodland Cemetery, there is a gathering of equally famous people, including Paul Laurence Dunbar, the first black poet to win renown in the United States and a friend of the Wright brothers, the guys who built the first airplane. The Wright brothers are also buried here, as is Charles Kettering, the man who prevented countless broken arms by inventing the self-starter for cars. Test pilot Frank Patterson rests here; it was a plane crash that took his life. His name lives on as the "Patterson" of Wright-Patterson Air Force Base. There is another Patterson buried here, and he is responsible for cash registers all over the world. John Patterson founded the National Cash Register Corporation.

In the nearby Miami Valley Memory Gardens at 1639 E. Lytle-Five Points Road in Dayton, you will find the grave of a man who had a profound effect on the world—Ermal C. "Ernie" Fraze. He was the inventor of the "pull tab" that opens countless cans of beer and soft drinks.

Longest Covered Bridge in the U.S.

ASHTABULA TOWNSHIP

Ashtabula County is home to the longest covered bridge in the United States. The **Smolen-Gulf Bridge** stretches 613 feet across—and a dizzying 93 feet above—the Ashtabula River on State Route 25. It was completed in 2008 at a cost of eight million dollars. A whopping 613,000 board feet of lumber were used in its construction (as well as seven million pounds of concrete and a half-million pounds of steel for the bridge's piers and abutments). There is a five-foot-wide covered walkway on each side of the bridge.

Why build a wooden covered bridge in the twenty-first Century? Believe it or not, covered bridges made of wood hold up better over the years than steel bridges. Several wooden bridges still being used in Ashtabula County are more than 100 years old. The Smolen-Gulf Bridge brings the total number of covered bridges in Ashtabula County to 17, including four other new ones built since 1983. The Ashtabula County Convention and Visitors' Bureau (1850 Austinburg Rd., Austinburg; 800-337-6746) has a map of the bridges.

The Big Easy of Austinburg

AUSTINBURG

Remember the song, "Ol' rockin' chair's got me. . ."?

Rocking chairs seem to have a special place in the hearts of Americans, from the time we are rocked in one as a baby until the sunset of our lives, when we rock away the time that is left to us. But perhaps no rocking chair is as special as this one alongside the highway in Austinburg.

The chair, which stands about 25 feet high, is currently an advertisement for a furniture company that owns the site, but over the years it has been owned by several other firms, including a lumberyard and a video store.

The present owner told me the chair had been built sometime

in the 1960s or '70s, and a previous owner had assured him that the chair was listed in a book of records somewhere as the **"World's Biggest Boston Rocking Chair."**

Maybe it is. At least I couldn't find any listings for bigger giant Boston rocking chairs. If you're out Austinburg way, judge for yourself. The chair is located on the west side of State Route 45, at the north end of the village of Austinburg.

Garden Tools for Giants

BAY VILLAGE

It may appear that you've stumbled upon Paul Bunyan's garden at the rear of the **Lake Erie Nature and Science Center** (28728 Wolf Rd., Bay Village; 440-871-2900) in Bay Village, Ohio. There, leaning against the roof of the building, is a lawn rake nearly 15 feet long, and standing beside it are a watering can big enough to water several acres of flowers and a pail big enough to carry a young boy. Visitors to the Nature and Science Center have been posing with the over-sized tools for years. They were once a part of another museum's Peter Rabbit's Garden exhibit. When the exhibit closed, the Bay Village center purchased the king-size tools and placed them in its nature exhibit.

Behalt

BERLIN

Heinz Gaugel had a dream. A rather big dream. He was an artist, and the masterpiece he dreamed of turned out to be a painting 10 feet tall and 265 feet long.

Gaugel, a German soldier in World War II and former prisoner of war held by the Americans, was rebuilding his life in his new country, Canada. He was a self-taught painter, and his work was starting to draw attention, especially his large murals.

While traveling in the early 1960s, Gaugel happened to stop in Berlin, Ohio. At the time he was unaware of the Amish and Mennonite people, but he did recognize the fact that these plainly dressed folk spoke German.

Heinz was so captivated by the Amish and their ways that he decided to stay and tell their story in a huge painting.

This was no easy matter. The Amish, as part of their religion, shun photos and likenesses of themselves. According to Paul Miller of the Mennonite Information Center, the Amish have seen their beliefs twisted and used for personal gain by others who came to the farming community and wanted to exploit them, so Heinz at first got very little help or encouragement from them.

However, he delved into the history books and did such a good research job that by the time he started to paint his mural, he had impressed many of the locals with his sincerity.

To some he was "that crazy German" who worked to the sound of Beethoven in an old one-room schoolhouse at the corner of U.S. Route 62 and Mt. Hope Road. He had a canvas stretched all the way around the room. Books were everywhere, and standing on the floor he would use a long stick with a charcoal pencil at the end to sketch in the figures that he would later paint.

"That crazy German" spent 14 years creating one of the world's largest cycloramic paintings in tiny Berlin, Ohio.

He worked for 20 years on the painting. It was completed in 1992. He called it *Behalt*, which means "to hold" or "to remember." The giant circular painting is mounted in a specially built circular room at the **Amish & Mennonite Heritage Center** (5798 County Road 77, Berlin; 330-893-3192). It is considered one of only a half-dozen cycloramic paintings in the world and one of the biggest. What is more incredible is that Gaugel did it all by himself. He hired no other painters to help. It was almost an obsession in the last third of his life. And the most wonderful thing is that his work is appreciated by the Amish and the Mennonites. It is not unusual to see groups of Amish children being led around the room, gazing at a painted mural of their history.

Gaugel later painted a series of regular-sized paintings that portrayed American folk heroes like Johnny Appleseed, and he did several religious works. He was working on one when he died on December 28, 2000, at the age of 73.

World's Largest Amish Buggy

BERLIN

What do you do if you are opening a new business in the heart of the world's largest Amish community and you want to get the attention of the tourists?

Obviously, you build a giant buggy.

That, at least, is what the owners of **Wendell August Forge** (U.S. Rte. 62, Berlin; 330-893-3713) did.

Their buggy sits in the middle of a barn-like showroom. Its front wheels alone are 5 feet high; the entire buggy is 7 feet, 4 inches wide and 10½ feet high. The driver's seat is up about as high as the seat in a tractor-trailer rig. It would take a horse about twice the size of a Clydesdale to pull the vehicle.

A Chair for God

BERLIN

God has a chair waiting for him in Holmes County.

In 1849 Jonas Stutzman, the first Amish settler to arrive in eastern Holmes County, published a booklet in which he predicted that God was about to return sometime within the next four years.

To get ready for the big event, Stutzman wore nothing but white clothing. He was so convinced God was coming that he built an oversized chair for the Lord's exclusive use. The chair was constructed with perfectly fitted parts, and not one nail was used in it.

Stutzman's forecast did not come true, but at one time he had many fellow believers.

An unusual man to the end, when he died in 1871 Stutzman requested that his body not be carried in any kind of vehicle. So at his funeral his fellow church members formed two alternating teams of pallbearers who carried his casket by hand seven miles to the hillside family cemetery in Walnut Creek.

You can see Stutzman and his chair depicted in the mural *Behalt* at the **Amish & Mennonite Heritage Center** (5798 County Road 77, Berlin; 330-893-3192) in Berlin, Ohio. The actual chair that Stutzman built, "God's chair," is also on display at the center.

Fort Laurens and Ohio's Unknown Soldier

BOLIVAR

It's a little-known fact that Ohio had a small part in the Revolutionary War. In what was then wilderness frontier, Fort Laurens was built in 1778 and named in honor of Henry Laurens, then president of the Continental Congress.

It was an ill-conceived plan to build a fort so far from the Continental Army's supply lines. The idea was to wage a campaign to attack the British at Detroit. But between the banks of the Tuscarawas River at Bolivar, where Fort Laurens was located, and Detroit were hundreds of fierce Native Americans loyal to the British.

The British and the Indians easily cut the supply lines and surrounded the fort.

The starving garrison was surrounded and under siege for more than a month before being forced to abandon the fort in 1779.

Today there is just a faint outline where the fort once stood. The Ohio Historical Society maintains the **Fort Laurens State Memorial** (open Apr.–Oct., Fort Laurens Rd., Bolivar; 800-283-8914) on part of the land where the fort was. Remains of the soldiers who died defending the fort are buried in a crypt in the museum. Except for one.

In the 1970s, while repairs to a parking lot at the museum were being done, another body was found—the body of an American officer who had died fighting at Fort Laurens. It was decided that he would become Ohio's own "unknown soldier," and he was buried with full military honors in an above-ground crypt in the middle of the park. The inscription on his grave reads, "Tomb of the Unknown Patriot of the American Revolution."

There's only one problem. Later research uncovered his identity, and researchers now say they know who's buried in the tomb of the "Unknown Patriot." (So far, though, there are no plans to make any changes to the tomb.)

Howl with the Wolves

BOLIVAR

A wolf was last seen running wild in Ohio back around 1850. After that, most of them headed for less populous states.

But Marty Huth has always had a fascination with wolves, so he applied to the U.S. Fish and Wildlife Service and obtained a permit to raise his own pack of wolves for an educational program, which he named **Wolf Timbers** (866-874-9653).

It operates on about 30 acres on a remote wooded hillside. A path leads you down through the woods to an 8-foot-high fence. Once inside here you can see a smaller area, about one acre in size, that is also fenced in. In there are the wolves—three of them, two males and a female.

Bleachers and an elevated deck for wheelchairs outside the fence are as close as visitors get to the wolves. Marty instructs them not to make eye contact with the wolves (wolves perceive that as a threat), to be quiet (wolves are frightened by humans), and not to eat in front of them (he doesn't want wolves associating humans with food).

Marty asserts that there has never been a proven case of an unprovoked wolf attack on a human being. Reported attacks on pioneers were probably by packs of wild dogs, he says, not wolves. He

THE SILVER SPADE

CADIZ

The Silver Spade, one of the largest dragline shovels in the world, once worked in the coalfields of Harrison County.

How large was it? Well, it weighed 14-million pounds. Its shovel, in a single bite, could scoop up to 105 cubic yards—about 158 tons—of dirt and rock. Its boom stretched 200 feet into the air (the height of the first drop on Cedar Point's Magnum roller coaster). It could stand on the 50-yard line of a football field, pick up 158 tons in one end zone, swing it across the entire football field in one motion, and place it 45 feet beyond the goalpost at the opposite end. Pretty darned large.

The Silver Spade was built in the Ohio coalfields and started operating in November, 1965. Its job was to re-move dirt and rock above coal seams so that miners could more easily reach the coal.

Most people couldn't appreciate its size, because you could only see the Silver Spade occasionally from the roadside, working far in the distance. But when it changed location and had to cross a road. Then, it dwarfed large trucks and even the roadway itself, and you see just how big it really was.

In early 2007, efforts to raise funds to turn the retired machine into a memorial failed and demolition work was started. The Silver Spade is now just Ohio history.

Q: Why did the Silver Spade cross the road?
A: Does a 14-million-pound vehicle need a reason?

also reminds visitors that a wolf is a wild animal and would make a lousy pet.

Sometimes Marty and his volunteers start to howl like a wolf, and the wolves join in. It's sort of a backwoods sing-along, wolf-style. The wolves seem to love it and become very active, leaping on fallen trees, throwing back their heads, and loosing hair-raising howls. It's such a popular part of the attraction that Wolf Timbers offers special "Howlnights" during the year when you can come and join in.

A Cannon with Whitewalls

BRIGHTON

Brighton is just a crossroads, a wide spot in the highway between the village of Wellington on the east and the town of Bellevue on the west. But in the fervor following victory in World War II, local veterans wanted a memorial to their service and petitioned the government for a piece of equipment—a used tank, perhaps, or a fighter plane—something that would honor the men and women of the community who had answered their country's call to arms.

What they got was kind of a disappointment at first. It was a small cannon with two rather dingy black rubber tires. The cannon also needed a paint job. It was chipped and rusting, as though it had been lying around a supply yard somewhere (which it probably had).

Brighton at that time was mostly made up of farm folks, and farm folks know how to make do. It's a way of life. So they hid their disappointment, cleared a patch of land, raised a flagpole, and put in a cement foundation for the little cannon. It looked like thousands of other small community parks.

Which wasn't quite enough, apparently, for some local citizens.

Right after World War II everyone wanted their cars to have fancy white sidewall tires. It was all the rage, especially with high school students. Some folks in Brighton say it must have been those high school students; perhaps some of the young veterans also helped. In any event, folks woke up one morning to find their cannon sporting bright white sidewall tires. It did give the gun a rather jaunty look. Some even said the whitewalls sort of softened the image of war that the cannon fostered. Anyway, the whitewalls were left on the cannon, and today many passersby still do a double-take when they see what is perhaps the only cannon in America with whitewall tires.

The **Brighton cannon** can be seen at the intersection of State Routes 511 and 18.

A King Was Born Here

CADIZ

His neighbors in Cadiz weren't overly proud of Clark Gable until he became a big-time actor known as the "King of Hollywood." Even then, they let his birthplace be torn down.

William Clark Gable was born on February 1, 1901, in an upstairs apartment of a home on Charleston Street. Five months after his birth, the family moved to a house on Lincoln Avenue.

Gable grew up in Harrison County, and when he was 17 he moved with his father first to Akron to work in the rubber industry and later out west to try his hand in the oil fields. Then he got discovered and went on to have a movie career that lasted several decades.

Even after Gable's death in the 1960s, little was done to celebrate his connection to Cadiz. His birthplace had been razed, and local folks were hard pressed to even point out where it had been.

Cadiz isn't shy about honoring folks. For a while in the early part of the last century, General George Armstrong Custer was the favorite son of Cadiz—even though he was actually born in New Rumley. Custer was memorialized in a hotel that bore his name, as well as by

Is this Clark Gable's busboy jacket?

several businesses. (The citizens of New Rumley put a large statue of Custer on the site where his house once stood—it seems the birthplaces of historical figures aren't highly prized in Harrison County.)

Cadiz began to think about capitalizing on one of their famous native sons in the early 1980s, when the town was suffering economically because of a downturn in demand for high-sulfur coal. A local group started holding a birthday celebration to honor Gable. It raised enough funds to buy a memorial marker to put on the property where Gable's birthplace once stood.

They chose the birthplace despite the fact that Gable had lived in the house for only about five months and had no memories of it. And despite the fact that his boyhood home, where he did spend most of his youth, was still standing nearby, the local group decided to launch a campaign to rebuild the Gable birthplace.

Many birthday parties later, the house was re-created. They even convinced Gable's only son, John Clark Gable, to come from California to cut the ribbon and tour the reconstructed four-room, second-floor apartment now known as the **Clark Gable Foundation** (138 Charleston St., Cadiz; 740-942-4989).

Maybe It's Something About the Water in Harrison County

CADIZ

Maybe it's something in the water, but a whole lot of famous or near-famous people have been born in, or lived in, Harrison County, Ohio. Leading the pack is Clark Gable (see, "A King Was Born Here"). Way back in 1938, a national radio show proclaimed Cadiz the "Proudest Little Town in America" because they had such a large number of well-known people who started their lives there.

The list included General George Armstrong Custer; Thomas Ward Custer (the only man to ever win two Congressional Medals of Honor in the same war); Edwin Stanton (Lincoln's secretary of war); Denton T. (Cy)

Young (Baseball Hall of Fame pitcher); General Thomas M. Vincent (Civil War general who delivered news of Lincoln's death to Vice President Andrew Johnson, and later ambassador to Japan); Ed Onslow (another Baseball Hall of Famer); and Edward Rensi (one time president of McDonald's).

There are even more names, but you get the idea. This is fertile ground for the birth of people who are destined to be leaders. Problem is, most of them left and never returned to their roots.

The **Harrison County Courthouse** (100 W. Market St., on the square in Cadiz) displays plaques honoring many famous local sons and daughters.

Those Crooked Bridges

CAMBRIDGE

Why would anyone want to build a crooked bridge?

Early settlers sometimes did, and several such bridges can still be found in West Virginia, Pennsylvania, and Ohio. More commonly called "S" bridges, they were designed by early bridge builders who found they could economically cross a stream, particularly one that the road hit on an angle, by making their bridge with curves.

It took less material and time to build a bridge shaped like an S so that the road crossed the stream at a true perpendicular, making the actual water crossing much shorter and, therefore, less expensive. However, this was in the days of horses and wagons, not fast-moving automobiles. Many of these bridges survived well into the twentieth century, and the walls bear the latter-day scars caused by motorists who suddenly, at high speed, found themselves fishtailing across the curvy bridges.

The best examples can be found along the old **National Road** (Old U.S. Rte. 40 between Cambridge and New Concord, Ohio) that ran from western Pennsylvania through West Virginia and into Ohio. We found two of the bridges still standing but now cordoned off as roadside parks, no longer carrying traffic.

First Ladies' Library

CANTON

Every U.S. president since Rutherford B. Hayes has had a presidential library dedicated to him. But what about their wives?

First ladies, of course, aren't elected. But they do happen to be the bed-mates of presidents, and that gives them an extraordinary perspective on history. What if a first lady kept a diary? What if she

didn't agree with her husband? What if she suspected him of "fooling around"? Well, the possibilities are endless, but the reality is that taxpayers or even large donors probably wouldn't spend the money to build twin libraries or museums for a first couple.

Well, now they don't have to. We have the **National First Ladies' Library** (331 Market Ave. S., Canton; 330-452-0876). It's located in the childhood home of former first lady Ida McKinley, wife of our 25th president, William McKinley.

Ida Saxton McKinley lived in this home before and after she married William McKinley. In fact it's the only home connected with the McKinleys still standing in Canton. The home they were living in when he was elected president was torn down years ago to make way for a hospital, and today the site is home to the county library.

The National First Ladies' Library operates an Internet site that collects all the information that can be found about the women who once served as first ladies of the land. The actual library contains a large assortment of books, many out of print, that have been written about the women. There is also a museum that contains a collection of photos, paintings, and other memorabilia belonging to the first ladies.

The Longest-Serving Police Car

CANTON

You can find the darnedest things in museums. At the **Canton Classic Car Museum** (555 Market Ave. S., Canton; 330-455-3603) you can see a 1937 Studebaker police car that may well be the longest-serving police car in U.S. history.

During the Great Depression, the city of Canton decided to purchase an armored police car. The reason depends on which story you hear. Maybe a bullet-proof vehicle was called for by Canton's growing reputation as a "Little Chicago" with lots of gangsters passing through. Or maybe it was because an understaffed police force needed the armored vehicle to deal with the strike violence that was associated with the labor movement in the 1930s.

Either way, the city purchased the car in 1937 for $800, a nominal price for a new car during the 1930s, and immediately spent an additional $4,600 on armor protection. That included three thousand pounds of ten-gauge steel plating and windows of one-and-an-eighth-inch-thick bullet-resistant glass with portholes so the officers could shoot safely at desperados and criminals from inside the tank-like car. They even wrapped the gasoline tank in a steel cocoon and replaced the wheels with double walled tires that could not be easily flattened by bullets.

But in their haste to make the car bullet-proof, the designers forgot to include anything for the comfort of the officers who had to drive the auto. The car had no ventilation and, of course, no air conditioning.

For most of its career, the car, which local police dubbed the "Flying Squadron," was used to transfer large sums of money between businesses in Canton.

In 1958, however, it proved its worth in dramatic fashion.

Two armed and dangerous robbers had holed up in a farmhouse near Louisville, Ohio and were holding an entire family hostage.

The standoff between the crooks and the local sheriff's department had gone on for over a day when the exasperated sheriff put in a call to Canton for the Flying Squadron. According to printed reports from that day, the big, black armored car came roaring down the driveway through a hail of bullets and pulled up in front of a window in the home. Police fired tear-gas canisters out through the portholes and into the house. Within moments, the robbers surrendered and the family was safe.

The armored car continued to serve Canton until 1996, when it was retired and donated to the Canton Classic Car Museum. By that time it had been on active duty for a remarkable total of fifty-nine years.

The First Highway

CANTON

Next time you sit cursing in bumper-to-bumper traffic on the highway, remember that at one time there weren't even any interstates.

If, say, you wanted to go from the east coast to the west coast, once you left the city streets you found yourself at first on gravel and then ordinary mud paths that were supposed to be roads. Many were unmarked, and it was anyone's guess exactly where you were or where you were headed.

As you got farther west, farther away from the cities and the farms, the roads just stopped, and, at the very best, you might have a trail or smooth area to follow. In short, driving was pretty much restricted to the cities, where they at least had paved streets.

A man by the name of Carl Fisher wanted to change all that. Fisher was president of an Indiana firm called Prest-O-Lite (he was also creator of the Indianapolis Motor Speedway).

Fisher wanted to build a coast-to-coast rock

road, and to do it he turned to two Ohio men: Frank Seiberling, president of Goodyear in Akron, and Henry Joy, president of the Packard Motor Car Company, which had started in Warren. Joy wanted to name the highway in honor of Abraham Lincoln. He was named president of the Lincoln Highway Association in 1913.

What they did was lay out a series of roads that connected cities, towns, and villages across 3,389 miles of America. It stretched from Times Square in New York City to Lincoln Park in San Francisco. It was to be America's first coast-to-coast paved highway. Building it wasn't easy. States, towns, and villages had to cooperate, and there was the question of who would pay for it. But it finally happened, and while a far cry from today's wide interstate expanses, it did tie the country together and provide the first transcontinental highway. It twisted and turned, was only two narrow lanes in many places, and was made of bricks or sometimes just gravel, but it was a highway, and it was marked. You could travel and see occasional markers identifying the highway to reassure you that you were not lost.

The Ohio section of the highway passed through eleven Ohio counties and seven county seats. In 1928, Boy Scouts in Ohio placed identifying cement markers along the highway. Only three remain today; they can be seen along U.S. Route 30 in East Canton, Mifflin, and near Dalton. If you are driving along U.S. Route 30 today and notice a road or highway sign that says **"Lincoln Way" or "Lincoln Road,"** it's part of the original **Lincoln Highway** that went coast to coast.

The Little Car from Ohio

CANTON

Right after World War II a couple of guys in Athens, Ohio, decided they wanted to create a new kind of automobile, one that was small and inexpensive and could be bought direct from the factory. They created the King Midget.

Believe it or not, their Midget Motors Corporation was the sixth largest manufacturer of automobiles in the United States for a number of years.

Claud Dry and Dale Orcutt wanted to design a car that anyone could afford. Their first was just a one-passenger model with a single-cylinder engine. Later versions seated two and were powered by 7.5 horsepower—about the same as garden tractors today.

They also added one other little touch. No dealers. You had to come to the factory to buy the car.

The later version of the car closely resembled early golf carts. In fact, they made a model that could be adapted to the golf course, and as an accessory you could have two golf-bag racks installed, and extra-wide tires for traveling over the turf.

The little car company survived for nearly twenty-five years, going through several owners and finally stopping production in 1970.

Today there are several King Midget automobile clubs, and you can see a typical model on display at the **Canton Classic Car Museum** (555 Market Ave. S., Canton; 330-455-3603).

Dead Man Talking

CANTON

President William McKinley may be dead, but he's still talking. The **McKinley Museum and National Memorial** (800 McKinley Monument Dr., Canton; 330-455-7043) has life-size animatronic versions of President and Mrs. McKinley. Enter a large second-floor room of this Victorian home, and you'll see what appears to be a couple of mannequins, frozen in time. But trigger an invisible beam and these lifelike First Figures start chatting away. It can be pretty unsettling for a first-time visitor. President McKinley comes alive!

The McKinleys patiently wait for their chance to startle another unsuspecting visitor.

The Fighting McCooks

CARROLLTON

Some families are just born to fight. I don't mean with each other. They're the kind of people that we are all very grateful for every time a war comes along.

Through the years there have been many cases of family members going off to war together. (Among the best known are the five Sullivan brothers who joined the Navy in World War II and all died while fighting on the same ship.) But the contributions of one Ohio family during the Civil War are hard to beat.

Major Daniel McCook of Carrollton went off to war accompanied by his nine sons and five nephews. They were rightly called "The Fighting McCooks."

Five members of the family became generals during the war.

Daniel McCook, at age 63, lost his life in the war; a son, Latimer McCook, a doctor, died of wounds he received in the war; another son, Charles McCook, also was killed in battle.

A son, Edwin Stanton McCook, one of the five promoted to general, became acting governor of Dakota and was assassinated there in 1873.

You can see the home and hear the story of The Fighting McCooks at the **McCook House and Civil War Museum** (Carroll County Historical Society, on the square in Carrollton; 800-600-7172).

The Blue Hole

CASTALIA

The Blue Hole in Castalia has been a bona fide Ohio tourist attraction for many years.

And it's just a hole in the ground, full of water. But people from all over America have paid money to come and see it.

What is so special about this particular hole in the ground? Maybe it's that everything in the hole, including the water, is sort of a blue-green color. Also, local legend has it that the hole has no bottom—anything that falls in just keeps right on going into the center of the earth.

The fact is, nobody has yet figured out just where the water does come from. The actual depth of the Blue Hole is about 70 feet. Through a small hole at the bottom, water from an underground source pushes its way to the surface, water that has no life in it—no oxygen—and that is constantly at 48 degrees, winter and summer. The Blue Hole never freezes.

About 7,500 gallons of that water gush from the earth every minute, filling both the Blue Hole and other nearby cavities and also spawning Cold Creek (which eventually runs into Lake Erie at Sandusky Bay).

NATURAL BRIDGES OF OHIO

It might surprise you to learn that Ohio, which is not exactly known for its mountains and valleys, has at least a dozen natural arches or bridges available to be admired by the public. These are usually made of rock that has been hollowed or undercut by rivers and lakes, and sometimes by prehistoric seas.

Some are not very big. But the Ohio Department of Natural Resources (2045 Morse Road, Columbus; 614-265-7095) says all of them do qualify as naturally formed bridges or arches. So here is a list of some of the more interesting and unusual ones.

Rockbridge, located in Hocking County, is, at 95 feet long, the largest of Ohio's natural bridges. It can be seen at the 212-acre Rockbridge State Nature Preserve near the town of Rockbridge, Ohio. It is located 1.5 miles from Rockbridge, southeast on U.S. Route 33; proceed south on Crawford-Starner Road (Township Road 504); then turn immediately east on Dalton Road (Township Road 503) and proceed 0.5 mile to the dead end. Parking and maps of the trail system are available.

Probably the smallest of the natural arches is located in the Lake Erie Islands, on Gibraltar Island, near South Bass Island. It is called Needle's Eye and is only 32 inches wide, but at least 15 feet tall, including part of it that is under water. The tiny opening is through a piece of dolomite, a sedimentary rock similar to limestone that makes up much of the Lake Erie Islands. It can be seen on the northeast end of Gibraltar Island at the mouth of the Put-in-Bay Harbor. It can be spotted from the Perry Peace Memorial on Put-in-Bay, but the only real way to see it up close is by boat.

What is likely the only natural bridge in Ohio that carried automobile traffic can be found near Marietta. The Ladd Natural Bridge is 40 feet long, 12 feet wide, and 5 feet thick. It spans a small waterfall on the side of a hill. Shortly after World War I, the Ladd family, who owned the property, tried to make a tourist attraction out of the bridge, charging 10 cents admission to view and walk over it. It's said some brave souls even drove their cars over the natural bridge, which has a 50-foot drop-off on one side. The area today is a state nature preserve. To visit it you must first apply to the Division of Natural Areas and Preserves for a free permit. They in turn will furnish you with maps to reach the bridge.

The Blue Hole is owned by a local fishing club that operated the attraction for several years as a sort of side business. Dwindling admission receipts and the cost of complying with the Americans with Disabilities Act proved too high, so the park around the Blue Hole was closed.

That seemed to be the end of the story. The Blue Hole was still there, behind locked gates still pumping 7,500 gallons of water a minute into Lake Erie, but the public could not see it.

Then came a discovery. The state of Ohio had purchased a fish hatchery next to the Blue Hole property to raise trout and other fish for Ohio streams. Part of the purchase included a second Blue Hole, about the same size as the original. The grass around it was mowed, some decking was put down on the marshy edges of the spring, and a new Blue Hole is now open to the public.

The water, which contains lime, soda, magnesium, and iron (that's what causes the blue color) encrusts just about everything, including moss and tree stumps that fall into the pool.

You can see the new Blue Hole year 'round Monday through Friday from 8 a.m. until 3 p.m. at **Castalia Fish Hatchery** (7018 Homegardner Rd., Castalia; 419-684-7499).

Fans of the legendary Blue Hole were saddened when the fishing club that owned it closed it to visitors. Then a new Blue Hole popped up right next door, and now the natural mystery is back in business.

Balto the Wonder Dog

CLEVELAND

There's a statue of Balto the Wonder Dog in New York's Central Park, but Cleveland's got the real thing.

He's dead, of course. In fact, he's been dead since 1933, when he passed on at the Cleveland Zoo. But he's still standing at the ready in the **Cleveland Museum of Natural History** (1 Wade Oval, Cleveland; 216-231-4600).

Who was Balto, and why was he so famous?

In 1925, Balto was just another Alaskan sled dog, when an epidemic of diphtheria broke out in Nome. Several children had died of the disease, and local doctors put out a radio message asking for life-saving antitoxin serum. It was midwinter, and in those days sled-dog teams were still relied on for transportation.

A hospital in Anchorage had the serum, but the state was in the midst of a blizzard. The serum went by train as far it could go, then sled-dog teams were to try relaying the precious medicine the rest of the way to Nome. It was a wild trip. Temperatures were at nearly 50 degrees below zero, and the wind was so vicious that dog-sled drivers could hardly see the trail.

The last 56 miles of the trip were the most severe. They had to pass over a frozen lake, with no markers to guide them. In addition, Gunnar Kaasen, the driver, was rendered temporarily blind by the blowing snow particles and so had to rely totally on the directional instinct of his lead dog—Balto.

The team made it in time to save many children. The story was picked up by news media around the world, and the dogs, especially Balto, became international heroes.

So many people wanted to see the spunky little dogs that it was arranged for them to tour the United States. But fame is fleeting, and before they got back home the tour ran out of money. The dogs were sold to a vaudeville promoter, and that seemed to be the end of the story—until in 1927 Cleveland businessman George Kimble, visiting California, found the dogs on display in a rundown, filthy exhibition hall. The dogs were sick and ill-kept. Kimble came back to Cleveland and started a campaign to save the animals. Cleveland schoolchildren donated pennies and nickels, and residents also chipped in to raise $2,000, a very large sum in those days. It was the asking price for Balto and the team. They were brought back to Cleveland and given a home at the Cleveland Zoo for the rest of their lives.

Balto died in 1933, and, in tribute to his heroism, he was stuffed and mounted and put on display at the Cleveland Museum of Natural History.

Oh, and in death he finally did get back home—briefly. He was loaned to Alaska a couple of years ago to be part of a program about the rescue. But after a short visit Balto came back to Cleveland.

Today he only makes occasional appearances for groups of youngsters, usually around the anniversary of the great rescue. Call the museum to see if Balto is scheduled to be on the job.

The story was picked up by news media around the world, and the dogs, especially Balto, became international heroes.

Free Stamp
CLEVELAND

One person's art is another person's . . . well, you finish the sentence.

Not all of us share the same aesthetic.

Take, for instance, the world's largest rubber stamp, er, priceless work of art—that stands in the shadow of Cleveland City Hall.

When the Standard Oil Company was building its headquarters on Cleveland's Public Square, it commissioned artist Claes Oldenburg to create a 28-foot-tall, 48-foot-wide steel sculpture shaped like a rubber office stamp, with the word "Free" on top, as the centerpiece of the new building's lobby. Before the stamp could be delivered, though, Standard Oil was sold to BP, and the new British management didn't seem to like the idea of having it anywhere near the building.

So the stamp was placed in storage in Indiana, and there it lay, forgotten, for the next seven years. Forgotten, that is, except by the BP officials who had to authorize the storage fees each month. In 1991 BP had finally had enough, and they offered to donate *Free Stamp* to the city of Cleveland as public art.

But city officials said, "No thanks"—they didn't like it much, either. Their attitude changed, however, when BP upped the ante and offered not only to give the stamp to the city but to pay for its installation, too. Suddenly it was much more attractive. And you might say that's how Cleveland got *Free Stamp* for free.

Free Stamp sits in **Willard Park** (Lakeside Ave., just east of City Hall, Cleveland).

Eliot Ness Comes Home

CLEVELAND

Eliot Ness, the "untouchable" from the 1950s TV series, was a real person and, for a part of his life, an Ohioan. And now he's spending eternity here.

Most of us associate Ness with Al Capone and the gangsters of 1920s Chicago. To be sure, Ness was there, but most of the stories we saw on television about Eliot Ness were just that, stories—a writer's fantasy, made up over the objections of Ness, who wanted just the facts told. Ness worked hard to bring down Capone, but the job was done mostly by accountants in the Treasury Department. The real Eliot Ness probably never carried a Thompson submachine gun, either. His career in Chicago was rather routine and attracted very little news media attention.

When Ness was done in Chicago, he came to Cleveland and became the city's safety director. He cleaned up the police department, ousting cops that were on the take, and he took on street gangs that were running out of control. He even cut traffic deaths enough to win awards for the city. But then he inexplicably left town to work for the federal government again, at the height of his popularity, rejecting calls that he run for mayor in 1941. (He did come back in 1946 and, against the advice of his friends tried to run for mayor, but by then too many years had gone by; he was badly beaten.) All in all, Ness did a far better job in Cleveland, and probably accomplished more good in Ohio than he ever did in Chicago, but that is not what he is remembered for.

In fact, Ness never saw himself become famous. He died of a heart attack in 1957, just as the book *The Untouchables* was being published. He was so uncertain that the book would be popular that he sold the rights to his story for just $300. He died never knowing that Hollywood was about to make him into a legend. Desilu Studios bought the story, and in 1959, with actor Robert Stack as Ness, they brought the story to the small screen.

Eliot died nearly broke, and at his request he was cremated. A few years later his ashes were joined by those of his last wife, Elisabeth, and adopted son, Robert, when they passed away. The three boxes of cremains wound up in the northern Ohio garage of a Ness family friend.

They sat there for nearly 40 years until Rebecca McFarland, a research librarian and vice president of the Cleveland Police Historical Society, got a tip. She managed to locate the family friend and convinced him to donate the cremains to the Police Museum on condition that they disperse them over water.

A plot at Lake View Cemetery was donated, and permission granted to spread the remains over Wade Lake there. A monument was also donated, and on Wednesday, September 10, 1997, Eliot Ness officially and finally came home to Cleveland as funeral services were held at the cemetery.

Ness the legend made millions of dollars for Hollywood, but Ness the man never benefited from his fame.

Besides the memorial in **Lake View Cemetery** (12316 Euclid Ave., Cleveland; 216-421-2665), you can also see an exhibit of some of Eliot Ness's personal belongings at the **Cleveland Police Historical Society and Museum** (Justice Center, 1300 Ontario St., Cleveland; 216-623-5055).

The Crime Eliot Ness Couldn't Solve

CLEVELAND

Among Ohio's most infamous unsolved crimes were the Torso Murders in Cleveland during the 1930s.

They baffled crime-fighter Eliot Ness, who was then the city's safety director. The murders eventually stopped, although no one was ever charged. There were 13 murders in all, mostly of unidentified people. All were decapitated and dismembered, possibly while they were still alive. The grisly chain of murders went on for four years.

In his desperation to solve the mystery, Ness took an unusual step.

In 1936 the Great Lakes Exposition,

A plaster head of the last victim is part of the Cleveland Police Historical Society and Museum's "Torso Murder" collection.

a sort of world's fair, was being held in Cleveland, and thousands of tourists were flocking to the city.

Ness was in the midst of trying to identify one of the most recent victims, a man in his twenties, who had been decapitated like the rest. He ordered a plaster mask made of the severed head and put it on display at the Great Lakes Exposition in hope that someone would recognize the man. Although more than 100,000 people gawked at the gruesome display, no one identified him.

That plaster head is still on display (along with the heads of three other victims) at the **Cleveland Police Historical Society and Museum** (Justice Center, 1300 Ontario St., Cleveland; 216-623-5055). The crimes are still officially unsolved.

One of the Largest Exhibition Buildings in the World

CLEVELAND

It's so big that you could drive a jumbo jet through the doors and onto the floor.

It's so big it has its own railroad spur; the line runs right through the center of the building.

It's so big, a giant Ferris wheel fits inside (just poking out through the roof).

It's the International Exposition Center—the I-X Center, for short. With nearly a million square feet of continuous exhibition space, the giant building is one of the largest single-structure exhibition buildings in the entire world.

You'd think Clevelanders would be plenty proud of owning such a facility.

The city can't wait to tear it down. They want the land for a runway expansion at neighboring Cleveland Hopkins Airport.

The I-X Center was erected back in 1942, specifically for building giant B-29 Superfortress bombers. Hence the big doors and enormous indoor space. At its peak it employed 15,000 workers.

During the Korean War, it was operated by General Motors, and army tanks were built there.

It was finally declared surplus in 1972, and the government sold the building in 1977 to the Park Corporation of Charleston, West Virginia, which in 1985 came up with the concept of making the old plant into a giant exhibition center. The hall became home to giant trade shows.

The land the building stands on, however, has been argued over for years. The city of Brook Park owned it (and raked in the taxes from it). The city of Cleveland wanted it for their airport. The two bickering burgs finally struck a deal in 2001, and the **I-X Center** (6200 Riverside Dr., Cleveland; 800-795-9690) is doomed to destruction around 2015.

Rock and Roll—Born in Ohio?

CLEVELAND

A lot of people claim that rock and roll was born in Ohio. It wasn't, but the name, at least, was coined there—by Cleveland disk jockey Alan Freed.

Freed was working at WXEL-TV (forerunner of FOX 8 TV) in 1951 when record store owner Leo Mintz talked him into playing some rhythm-and-blues records on WJW radio. (At that time rhythm and blues was associated solely with African-Americans.) Freed, calling himself "Moondog," took over the show and was a hit.

In March 1952 Freed sponsored a dance, called the Moondog Coronation Ball, at the 10,000-seat Cleveland Arena. He invited many of the black rhythm-and-blues performers to entertain. An estimated crowd of nearly 20,000 showed up, the overflow crowd crashed the gates, and police had to cancel the dance. Nevertheless, this is considered the first rock concert.

In 1954, Freed moved on to New York City, where he staged another concert with many of the same performers, who were now called rock-and-roll artists. Within a month, the music industry was promoting rock-and-roll recordings across the country.

In the late 1950s Freed became embroiled in the payola scandal that shook up the radio business and he was fired from his broadcasting jobs. He died in Palm Springs, California, in January 1965. In 1986, Freed was among the original inductees into the **Rock and Roll Hall of Fame** (1 Key Plaza, Cleveland; 888-764-7625).

The Only Major League Baseball Player Killed on the Field

CLEVELAND

Raymond Chapman holds the distinction of being the only major league professional baseball player to be killed while playing the game.

Chapman, who played shortstop for the Cleveland Indians from 1912 to 1920, was hit by a ball pitched by Carl Mays of the New York Yankees, at the Polo Grounds on August 16, 1920. He died 12 hours later in a New York hospital. His death came at a time when the Indians were making their first real bid for a championship. Thousands turned out for his funeral at the Cathedral of St. John the Evangelist in downtown Cleveland.

His teammates dedicated the rest of the season to him and went on to win their first league and world championships.

Chapman is buried in **Lake View Cemetery** (12316 Euclid Ave.,

Cleveland; 216-421-2665), where baseball fans decorate his grave each year with baseball bats, gloves, and Cleveland Indians memorabilia.

Rocket Man

CLEVELAND

Drivers on Cleveland's East Side often report seeing a large silver rocket ship zooming up on them in their rear view mirrors.

It's not a hallucination. It's Ron Heitman of South Euclid.

If they take a second look, nostalgic motorists may recognize the shiny rocket from its earlier days hanging on cables at Cleveland's long-gone Euclid Beach Park.

Back then, three rockets flew in circles around a tall tower. Each car could seat 12 people. The park closed in 1969, and in 1978 Heitman came across one of the 28-foot-long rocket cars, bought it, and put it in his garage, not sure what to do with it.

In the mid-1970s, he arrived at the obvious conclusion: add a souped-up 455-horsepower Oldsmobile V8. With that, some wheels,

and an enlarged front compartment big enough for a driver and a steering wheel, he had a distinctive vehicle that could carry 10 people and travel at a top speed of 136 miles per hour.

He originally planned only to show the car in a few auto shows, but it was such a success that he started getting calls (216-382-1616) to be in parades—including the Macy's Thanksgiving Day parade and the Indianapolis 500 parade. Then there were the wedding parties and others that wanted to rent the car. He's become so busy with the vehicle that he finally tracked down another of the original rocket cars and has built his second rocketmobile.

The Only Fully Intact WWII Submersible

CLEVELAND

If we ever go to war with Canada, Ohio is ready.

We have the only fully intact, nearly operational World War II fleet submarine, the **U.S.S. Cod** (docked near the E. 9th St. pier, open May–Sept.).

Of course the shallow depth of Lake Erie might make maneuvering difficult. But on the other hand, since the most threatening boat on the Canadian side is probably a fishing trawler, odds are we won't have to try it.

The *Cod* has called the Cleveland lakefront home since 1959, when it was towed to Ohio to become a Naval Reserve training vessel. It was decommissioned in 1954, stricken from the navy's official inventory in 1971, and seemed headed for the scrap pile when a group of Clevelanders petitioned the navy to give them the ship for use as a World War II memorial.

The navy wasn't convinced until Parma Heights restaurant owner Johnny Tarr entered the picture. Tarr, a Hungarian immigrant who had fought for Germany in the war, turned over his restaurant one weekend to the sub preservation committee. He donated the food and labor; the proceeds went to the committee. It wasn't only the money, it was the publicity the act attracted that finally did the trick. On January 25, 1976, the navy turned the *U.S.S. Cod* over to the

Cleveland Coordinating Committee to Save the *Cod*, allowing it to become a memorial ship.

By the way, the *Cod* is an authentic war veteran. It sank more than a dozen enemy ships, including the Japanese destroyer *Karukaya*, in 1944, and also rescued the crew of a Dutch submarine that had to be abandoned in the South China Sea in 1945.

There's an interesting bit of trivia about the *Cod*. There was one piece of machinery aboard so important that the crew considered it impossible to patrol without: an ice-cream machine.

It may sound silly, but to young men crammed into small spaces, living under the sea for weeks and months at a time, ice cream was a real morale builder. The ice-cream maker on the *U.S.S. Cod* had been inoperable since the ship was mothballed in the 1950s. But in keeping with efforts to restore the ship as nearly as possible to its original condition, curator John Fakan worked out a deal with Lorain County vocational students. (They fixed the machine, and ate the first batch of ice cream it produced in 50 years.) Ironically, now that it's back on the sub, the ice-cream maker may never be used again, because it's in a museum. (By the way, the U.S. Navy was the only navy in the world to put ice-cream machines on submarines in World War II.)

HANG ON SLOOPY

State legislators perpetrated an act of musical silliness in 1985 when they decided we had to have an official "state rock song."

The song they chose was "Hang On Sloopy," written by Celina native Rick Derringer. It was first recorded by a Dayton rock band, the McCoys, in 1965.

House Concurrent Resolution No. 16 makes you wonder just how much useful business got done in the state legislature back in the 1980s. Just read a bit of the legislation passed to create the state rock song:

"WHEREAS, the members of the 116th General Assembly of Ohio wish to recognize the rock song "Hang On Sloopy" as the official rock song of the great state of Ohio, and

"WHEREAS, if fans of jazz, country-and-western, classical, Hawaiian, and polka music think those styles also should be recognized by the state, then by golly, they can push their own resolution just like we're doing.

"WHEREAS, "Hang On Sloopy" is of particular relevance to members of the Baby Boom Generation, who were once dismissed as a bunch of long-haired, crazy kids, but who now are old enough and vote in sufficient numbers to be taken quite seriously, and

"WHEREAS, adoption of this resolution will not take too long, cost the state anything, or affect the quality of life in this state to any appreciable degree, and if we the legislature just go ahead and pass the darn thing, we can get on with more important stuff . . ."

When Irish Eyes Are Smiling

CLEVELAND

Probably the most famous and popular Irish melody in the world was written by a Cleveland native who had never been to Ireland.

Ernest R. Ball, the composer of "When Irish Eyes Are Smiling," also wrote another Irish melody that we frequently hear on St. Patrick's Day, "Mother Machree," and he penned "A Little Bit of Heaven," another tune much loved by the Irish.

Ball never got to see the Emerald Isle. He died of a heart attack in 1927 and was buried in **Lake View Cemetery** (12316 Euclid Ave., Cleveland; 216-421-2665).

The Man Behind the Trophy

CLEVELAND

The Heisman Trophy has been awarded to the best player in college football annually since 1935. I suspect there are more than a few people (including some of its recipients) who have no idea who it is named after.

In 1869, **John William Heisman** was born in what is now Ohio City on Cleveland's west side. He grew up to be both a football player and a coach. Among the schools he coached was Oberlin College. Yes, that Oberlin College—the one that rarely wins today. Heisman also coached at more than a half-dozen major universities. He changed the face of football forever with such innovations as the forward pass, center snap of the football, audible signals to begin offensive play, and, some say, the creation of the "T" formation.

It was during his retirement years, while he was president of the New York Touchdown Club, that awards were handed out for the first time to the nation's best college football players. After his death, the main award was renamed in his honor and today is synonymous with the best of the best in football.

His birthplace in Ohio City has a historic marker (2825 Bridge Avenue, Cleveland; the home is privately owned).

The Father of CB Radio
CLEVELAND

Timing is everything.

Al Gross of Cleveland was a tinkerer. He was fascinated by radio. While he was in his teens he was a ham radio operator and invented the first walkie-talkie two-way radio. (It inspired Chester Gould, creator of the cartoon strip *Dick Tracy* to include a wrist-mounted two-way radio in the comic strip.)

During World War II, Gross worked for military intelligence and developed two-way radios used by spies and resistance fighters. After the war, Gross thought that there should be a wireless radio for the common man, so he invented that, too: citizens band, or CB, radio.

In 1949, a friend at a hospital told him about the problem of reaching doctors by telephone. Gross went to his workbench and came up with the first pager. But when he attended a conference of physicians that year, expecting them to make this invention a smashing success, he was met with a total lack of interest. One doctor told him that he couldn't understand why any physician would want such a product—especially on the golf links on their afternoon off. The first pager was a commercial flop. It was too far ahead of its time.

It was much the same story with Gross's other inventions. His key copyrights expired in early 1970, long before the electronic revolution. So when CB radios became the rage, Gross didn't see a penny. Back in the 1950s, he tried to interest telephone companies in an idea he had for a wireless mobile phone. They didn't listen.

Al Gross was always the right man, with the right invention . . . at the wrong time.

So other than lots of awards and plaques that call him the "father of two-way radio," he didn't get much out of his inventions, and Al Gross spent his life working for other people.

Life Savers
CLEVELAND

If you've ever enjoyed those little round candies with the hole in the middle, you can thank an Ohioan.

Back in 1891, Clarence Crane started manufacturing chocolates in Cleveland. But in those pre-air-conditioning days, chocolate sales sagged in the summer. (Chocolate gets pretty messy above 80 degrees.) Crane began experimenting with hard candy shaped like little life preservers. He called them Crane's Pep-O-Mint Life Savers. They became popular, and soon he was selling them year 'round.

A New York company bought out Crane's Life Savers trademark in 1913, paying him just $2,900 for the name and the recipe.

But don't feel too sorry for Clarence. His chocolate business continued to grow nationwide, making him very successful by the time of his death in 1931.

He also was the father of poet Hart Crane.

The Baseball Thrown From Outer Space
CLEVELAND

Back in Game Five of the 1995 World Series between the Cleveland Indians and the Atlanta Braves, history was made. No, the Indians didn't win the series. But they did start the game with a ball thrown from outer space. Here's how it worked. Space shuttle *Columbia* was on a mission to the International Space Station. Astronaut commander Ken Bowersox tossed a ball toward a camera in the shuttle, and his throw was televised on a large screen at Jacobs Field in Cleveland. As the image of the ball filled the screen, another ball was dropped from somewhere above into center field, and the game was on. One of the two balls is on display at the Baseball Hall of Fame in Cooperstown, New York; the other is on display in the Visitor Center at the **NASA Glenn Research Center** (21000 Brookpark Rd., Cleveland; 216-433-4000) in Cleveland.

The 13-Miles-per-Hour Speed Sign

COLUMBIANA

At the entrance to 66-acre **Firestone Park** (347 East Park Ave., Columbiana; 330-482-2656) in Columbiana is an unusual speed sign. It says "Speed Limit 13 MPH". Why 13, not the usual 10 or 15 miles per hour? A sign painter's mistake? A teen prank? Neither. The Columbiana police department says it is the legal speed limit for the park as approved by Columbiana city council, and if you go above 13 miles per hour while visiting the park you can be ticketed for speeding. It seems there had been problems with speeders in Firestone Park, so city council decided to set a limit. Both 10 and 15 miles per hour were suggested, but some argued that 15 was too fast and others said 10 was too slow. Finally in a flash of genius that would have made Solomon proud, someone on the council suggested splitting the difference and making it 13 miles per hour, pointing out that such an odd speed limit would probably catch people's attention.

North to Alaska . . . On a Tractor?
DALTON

You've heard the expression "a slow boat to China"? Well, how about an antique tractor to Alaska?

Glen and Betty Martin of Dalton drove their 1950 John Deere tractor, nicknamed "Dandelion," from their tiny Wayne County community to Alaska (and back!)—9,500 miles, average speed about 13 miles per hour. They took this astounding trip in 1998, pulling a small trailer behind the tractor for emergency shelter when they could not find any place along the way to stay.

The Martins, both in their sixties at the time, said they decided to make the trip as a way to spread their Christian faith. They wrote a book about it: *To Alaska On A Tractor*.

Buried in Three States
DOVER

One of the really bad guys of the American Civil War was an Ohioan, William Clarke Quantrill of Dover. Now, he may be the only American who is buried in three graves, in three different states.

Quantrill always had a mean streak. It is said that as a child he nailed snakes to trees, shot pigs through the ears to hear them squeal, and tied cats together by their tails to watch them fight. Even walking through farmers' fields as a boy, he was known to stab horses and slice open cows. The kind of kid that even gives juvenile delinquents a bad name.

During the Civil War, Quantrill joined the Confederate army in Missouri and took off with his own band of irregulars, the feared "Quantrill's Raiders" that savaged towns and villages in the West. He is most often remembered for the August 1863 sacking of Lawrence, Kansas, when his troop of 450 men tore through the community, pillaging, burning, and killing men, women, and children.

His career finally ended when he was shot and captured in a

battle in Kentucky. He died in a prison hospital in Louisville, Kentucky, and was buried in a cemetery there in 1865.

That's where *our* story actually begins.

In 1887, his mother and a boyhood friend visited the grave. She wanted the remains transferred to Dover, Ohio. The friend started digging, but when he unearthed the corpse he found it had disintegrated so badly that only a few bones and the skull were left. Most of his skeleton had turned to dust. Quantrill's mother identified the remains by a chipped tooth he had had since his youth.

The friend promised to transfer whatever bones he had found to Ohio, but he never got around to it.

The bones eventually ended up in the hands of the Kansas State Historical Society. In 1992, they gave one of Quantrill's arms and a shinbone to the Missouri Division of the Sons of Confederate Veterans, who buried them in the Confederate cemetery in Higginsville, Missouri. The skull went to the **Dover Historical Society** (325 E. Iron Ave., Dover; 330-343-7040), which had it interred (in a fiberglass child's coffin) in the Fourth Street Cemetery. Before it went back in the ground, though, a cast-clay replica of Quantrill's head was made from the skull. This was displayed at the historical society for a while, but during the hot days of summer, water would bead on the surface, making it look like the head was alive and sweating. This disconcerted some visitors so much that the head was removed to a refrigerator. Now it is shown only on request.

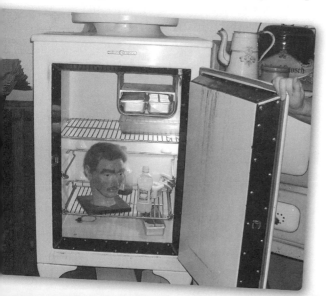

Quantrill's replicated head was moved to this refrigerator because it was sweating too much.

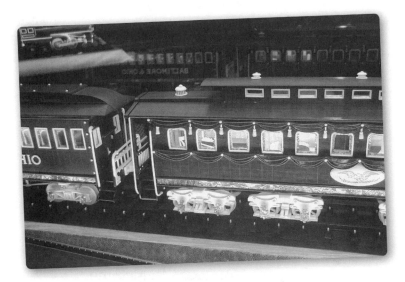

Ohio's Master Carver

DOVER

Ernest "Mooney" Warther is known throughout the state as "Ohio's master carver." His is a remarkable story. His father died when he was only two. He was forced to quit school after the second grade to help provide for his family. At age 28, while working at a steel company, he started carving. He used soup bones from his wife's kitchen, then switched to walnut.

Warther decided to carve the history of the steam engine. He carved 64 locomotives. And these weren't just solid carvings, but intricate models with moving parts. Tiny wheels turned, valves moved, pistons went up and down. Incredibly, he duplicated real locomotives in exact scale, down to the last rivet—without any plans and with essentially no formal education.

He carved, in miniature, the entire steel plant where he worked. He duplicated Abraham Lincoln's entire funeral train in ivory. He created ornate canes with caged balls in the handles. All done with a carving knife he had designed.

For amusement, Warther carved wooden pliers, first one pair, then a "tree" on which each branch folded out to form wooden pliers. The tree was a piece of black walnut 13 inches long, three-quarters of an inch wide, and five-eighths of an inch thick. Mooney calculated that if he made 31,000 cuts in the wood, he could create a tree with 511 pairs of working pliers when they were all folded out from the block of wood. He worked for nearly two months on the project, six to eight hours a day, before he completed it. It worked. It worked so well that it first appeared in *Ripley's Believe It Or Not* and then was loaned to the Ohio State Historical Museum in Columbus, where it was displayed for 14 years. Today it and many of Warther's other carvings are on display at the **Warther Museum** (331 Karl Ave., Dover; 330-343-7513).

Warther suffered a stroke while working on a steam locomotive called the *Lady Baltimore* and died in 1973 at the age of 87.

Funeral Memorabilia Museum

DOVER

John Herzig of Dover has one of the most unusual collections imaginable. He collects funeral memorabilia. He's got objects ranging from the original funeral director's papers outlining what Elvis and Vernon Presley wanted for Gladys Presley's funeral to the accordion from the iconic photograph of Franklin Delano Roosevelt's funeral. That accordion is believed to be the same instrument played by Coast Guard chief Graham Jackson as FDR's funeral train pulled out of the Warm Springs, Georgia, resort where he died. A photographer caught the memorable photo as Chief Jackson played "Going Home" on his accordion while tears streamed down his face. Jackson, a Coast Guard recruiter at the time, was also a talented musician and had been asked by FDR to play at many Warm Springs functions.

Herzig started the collection nearly 20 years ago as a hobby. He had planned to collect autographs, and one of the first that he found was one belonging to former heavyweight champion Joe Louis. But when he received the package with the autograph, it also included a program from Louis's funeral. Upon seeing that, Herzig, a third-generation funeral director, discovered a new hobby.

Since then he has amassed more than a thousand pieces of funeral memorabilia, including the visitation log for former New York Yankee manager Casey Stengel and mourning vests worn at the funeral of former U.S. president William McKinley.

Much of the collection is on display at the **Toland-Herzig Funeral Home** (803 N. Wooster Ave., Dover; 330-343-6132) in downtown Dover. It's open to the public, but it's always a good idea to call first so you can be sure your visit won't conflict with a funeral.

A Mortuary Museum/Bed-and-Breakfast

EAST LIVERPOOL

Here's one that really sets Ohio apart from other states. We have perhaps the only mortuary museum and bed-and-breakfast in the country.

It happened this way. Back in the mid-1930s, the infamous bank robber and murderer Charles "Pretty Boy" Floyd was number one on the FBI's most-wanted list. He was spotted while traveling near East Liverpool in October 1934 and finally trapped by a posse of local lawmen and FBI agents on a farm near the location of what is now Beaver Creek State Park. Floyd tried to run and was gunned down, bringing to an end his nefarious career.

Floyd's lifeless body was propped in the backseat of a police car and driven to Sturgis Funeral Home in East Liverpool. Frank A. Dawson, a funeral director working for Sturgis, took the bullet-riddled body into a basement preparation room for embalming.

Meanwhile word quickly spread through the small river town that "Pretty Boy" Floyd, America's number-one criminal, was dead, and that it had happened just outside of the city. Thousands of residents started to converge on the Sturgis Funeral Home. Everyone wanted to see the body. The crowd grew so large that an iron railing in front of the funeral home was torn from the ground. The lawn around the house was trampled.

The police, possibly fearing a riot, told funeral director Dawson to take the now-embalmed body into one of the viewing rooms and to let the people in.

Floyd was laid on a small bed in a center room on the first floor, his body partially covered by a blanket with only his shoulders and face visible. The doors were opened, and during the next three hours, from 8:30 until 11:30 that night, an estimated 10,000 people passed through the funeral home at a rate of about 50 per minute to catch a glimpse of the famous criminal.

The next morning Dawson shipped Floyd's body back to his family in Oklahoma, and things returned to normal in East Liverpool.

Today the former funeral home is owned by Frank C. Dawson, the son of the man who embalmed "Pretty Boy" Floyd. And the old Victorian home is now a bed-and-breakfast. **The Sturgis House** (122 W. 5th St., East Liverpool; 330-382-0194) has six bedrooms with private bath, one with whirlpool. Other amenities include a phone in each room, as well as television . . . and, of course, a breakfast room where "Pretty Boy" Floyd was once laid out.

If you ask, you can see the museum in the basement. The room has been left as it was in the 1930s when "Pretty Boy" Floyd was brought here. There are pictures on the wall of Floyd before and after the embalming. You can see the table where the work was done.

Some antique embalming equipment is also on display, as are several devices that were used under bodies to make them lie just so in a casket. If you're lucky, you might even get to meet Frank C. Dawson, who goes by the nickname "Digger." He and his family still operate a funeral home—just up the street.

A historical marker is located on Sprucevale Road, between East Liverpool and Rogers on the edge of Beaver Creek State Park. The site is the former Conkle family farm, where Charles "Pretty Boy" Floyd was shot down by police and FBI agents. The marker was erected in 1993 by the East Liverpool Historical Society and the Ohio Historical Society. It was stolen in 1995 and discovered lying in a wooded lot in East Liverpool several weeks later. It was reerected and has been unmolested since then.

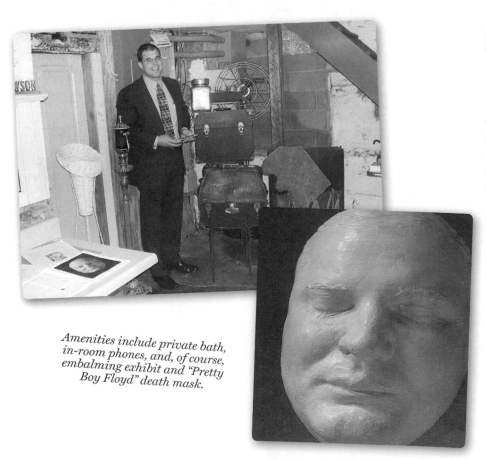

Amenities include private bath, in-room phones, and, of course, embalming exhibit and "Pretty Boy Floyd" death mask.

The Private Bridge over the Ohio River

EAST LIVERPOOL

To cross the Ohio River in East Liverpool, it will cost you either a nickel or four bits, depending on your mode of transportation.

Toll roads and toll bridges were once a way of life in our country. In the early days some bridges and even roads were privately owned, and people wanting to use them had to pay the toll or find some other way to cross the stream or swampy area.

But today about the only toll roads still operating are state-owned turnpikes and bridges. All, that is, but one down on the Ohio River.

The **Newell Bridge** that connects East Liverpool with Newell, West Virginia, was built way back in 1905 by the Homer Laughlin China Company, and today is still wholly owned by the firm. They built the bridge because after starting their company in East Liverpool, on the Ohio side of the river, they decided to move to Newell, West Virginia, just across the river for a bigger riverfront location. The problem was how to get their employees, who mostly lived in

Ohio, to work on time. The nearest public bridge was miles away.

So the decision was made to build a bridge over the Ohio River. Originally the bridge accommodated both trolleys and auto traffic, as well as pedestrians. Today the trolleys are gone, but nearly three thousand cars and trucks cross the bridge each day. Many of them carry Ohioans going across the bridge to reach the gambling casinos in West Virginia. And each car or truck pays 50 cents to cross the bridge. Pedestrians can walk across for only a nickel.

Otto Sirianni, the bridge manager, said that the tolls collected each year have been sufficient to maintain the bridge, and it has never had to be subsidized by anyone. The bridge floor was last replaced in 1954, but is inspected every spring for safety.

"Goth" in Ohio

EAST ROCHESTER

If you're a fan of *Frankenstein* (the book or the movies) or if you just adore Gothic architecture, you'll appreciate what a couple in East Rochester, Ohio, have created out of other people's castoffs and some ingenuity. **Stone Gate Manor** (10117 Mantle Rd. NE, East Rochester; 330-868-2834) is a replica of a 14th-century English manor house.

It has many spooky touches, including spires, stained-glass windows, and a large, forbidding gate.

It took William and Linda Cundiff almost eight years to build their Gothic dream house on a hillside they own near Minerva, Ohio. Sandstone rocks gathered from the 53-acre site were used for the walls. Wood for framing the house came from pine trees the Cundiffs had cut down and sawed into lumber. Hand-hewn beams for the ceilings were salvaged from an area barn that was being demolished. The couple also made their own stained-glass windows from salvaged bits of glass. They visited junkyards, flea markets, and even abandoned homes looking for furnishings and material to complete their 14th-century look.

The best part is that this Ohio oddity is open for tours by groups of 10 or more—by appointment, with an admission charge.

The Happiest Music on Earth

EUCLID

"The happiest music on earth" is what they call polka music. That must mean that the happiest musicians on earth are enshrined at the **National Cleveland-Style Polka Hall of Fame and Museum** (605 E. 222 St., Euclid; 216-261-3263).

Cleveland-style polka music has its roots in Slovenian folk music, but the influence of Cleveland's many other ethnic cultures has given it a distinctly American twist.

Songs like "Just Because Polka," "The Blue Skirt Waltz," "Slap Happy Polka," "I Wanna Call You Sweetheart Polka," "Little Fella Waltz," and "Old Timer's Polka" were born here.

The Polka King himself, Grammy award-winning Frankie Yankovic, is from Cleveland. He and other polka notables, like Walter Ostanek, Johnny Pecon, and the Vadnals—Frankie, Johnny, Richie, and Tony—are enshrined here.

Who Was the First President?

HARTSGROVE

Who was the first president of the United States? If you said George Washington, you might be wrong. At least as far as a Hartsgrove man is concerned.

When was the last time you saw John Hanson's picture on a $1 bill? Hanson was the first president of the United States elected under the Articles of Confederation. He was the first of eight men who served as president from 1781 until our current Constitution was adopted in 1789. As most people know, George Washington was the first president elected under the Constitution.

Nick Pahys, Jr., has spent most of his life studying the presidency, and he believes that all the presidents should be honored. So he has opened a presidential museum at his **Hartsgrove Emporium** (at the intersection of Rte. 6 and Rte. 534, Hartsgrove; 440-474-5369) that includes the eight presidents elected under the Articles of Confederation. It may be the only one that does.

Pahys has made it his life's work to get recognition for John Hanson. He claims the man was completely ignored for at least 150 years, since he wasn't even mentioned in encyclopedias until 1929.

In case you were wondering, the other seven who served before George Washington were Elias Boudinot, Thomas Mifflin, Richard Henry Lee, John Hancock, Nathaniel Gorham, Arthur St. Clair, and Cyrus Griffin.

HARBINGERS OF SPRING: BUZZARDS

HINCKLEY

In California, tradition has it that every March 19 the swallows return to the mission of San Juan Capistrano. That signifies the coming of spring.

Heck, swallows are just little, bitty things. Here in Ohio spring brings real birds—turkey vultures with six-foot wingspans. They head for Hinckley Township.

Here's how this tradition supposedly got its start. On December 24, 1818, the good citizens of Hinckley decided to have a really big hunting party. About 600 men and boys formed a wide circle around the township and starting walking toward the center, shooting and killing all the game they could find. When the day ended, the score was 300 deer, 17 wolves, 21 bears, and assorted fox, raccoons, and turkeys.

The hunters divvied up the best cuts of the meat, but they weren't very particular about what they did with the leftovers. Because it was winter, they just let the various carcasses lie on the ground to be covered by snow.

As long as the cold weather hung around and the snow kept falling, the scene probably looked just like one of those Currier and Ives paintings—a pioneer village under a mantle of white, smoke curling from the chimneys.

However, when March rolled around so did the spring thaw, and as the snow melted and the temperatures rose, Hinckley didn't look or smell so good.

The smell soon brought huge flocks of turkey vultures (some call them buzzards), who started doing their thing. It was quite a picnic for them, and eventually the turkey vultures were so well fed that they decided to hang around for the rest of the summer. And they started returning to Hinckley every year on March 15.

It took them a while, but a few enterprising folks in Hinckley eventually found a way to capitalize on this creepy phenomenon. About 150 years later, they were looking for a way to raise funds for the school, and someone suggested hosting a pancake breakfast on the same day that the buzzards return. With proper publicity, maybe city folks would come out to see this marvel of nature—and buy a pancake breakfast.

Boy did they ever. Today, the annual return of the buzzards to Hinckley is reported in the papers, on radio, on television, and in cyberspace. News media swarm into the Hinckley Reservation of the Cleveland Metroparks to the "official" buzzard watching station. People from all over America come to witness the phenomenon. Some even dress up like buzzards. Most have field glasses and telescopes that they train on the sky, watching crows and robins dart through the distant tree line. The movement of any feathered creature brings cries of "I see them!" and "There they are!" and everyone rushes to the fence, straining to share in the excitement of the moment.

Personally, I have covered the buzzards' return to Hinckley about 20 times in the last 30 years and have yet to see a real live buzzard flying over Hinckley Ridge. I did see one in a cage at the school where the pancakes are served, but he got there in the back of a park ranger's station wagon. Nevertheless, you will still find dozens and dozens of people each year at the ridge viewing area who would take an oath on their mother's life that they did indeed see the buzzards flying back to Hinckley.

If you want to see for yourself, call the Hinckley Chamber of Commerce (330-278-2066) for dates of the pancake breakfast. The buzzards, of course, are supposed to be there on March 15. Buzzard Roost is located at the corner of State Road and West Drive in the Cleveland Metroparks Hinckley Reservation.

By the way, my colleague Dick Goddard, the dean of Ohio television weathermen, pointed out that buzzards are notorious for regurgitating while they are flying. So never stand under a group of flying buzzards and look up.

Keep your eyes on the sky. Or just wait for one to show up in the back of the park ranger's station wagon.

World's Only Perambulator Museum

JEFFERSON

Twin sisters Judith Kaminski and Janet Pallo of Jefferson want to share their lifelong fascination with baby buggies.

Their **Victorian Perambulator Museum** (26 E. Cedar St., Jefferson; 440-576-9588) has the largest known collection of early wicker baby and doll carriages.

Modern foldable strollers give kids a lot more freedom, but some of the early baby buggies were pretty neat. For instance, one 1910 baby buggy was made to look like a Model T Ford. Another looks like a wicker gondola.

If you ever wondered what kids played with prior to the 20th century, the sisters also have a large collection of pre-1900 toys, sleds, and sleighs for children.

Open hours at the Perambulator Museum vary throughout the year, but it can also be toured by appointment. Just call first.

The Groovy Island

KELLEYS ISLAND

Kelleys Island in Lake Erie is truly groovy.

The island, the largest on the U.S. side of Lake Erie, displays very distinct grooves that were worn into it by a passing glacier.

This part of the earth was once covered by a giant ice floe. When it started to melt, around 18,000 years ago, the retreating ice dug deeply into the earth and stone that it passed over.

Kelleys Island is made up of solid limestone bedrock, and when the glacier passed over here it made very clear marks. One section of stone, about 430 feet long, 35 feet wide, and up to 15 feet deep, has escaped erosion and survived human interaction and still exists. Today it is fenced off as a national natural landmark.

Scientists think this grooved area was once much larger but was probably quarried away in the nineteenth century. It is located on the island's north side, adjacent to Kelleys Island State Park campground.

Queen Victoria's Bloomers

KENT

They probably won't show up in the pages of the Victoria's Secret catalog. They're not terribly sexy, or even attractive. But they're here in Ohio—an authentic pair of Queen Victoria's (blush) panties. Or, as they call them in England, knickers. Actually, I think they referred to them as bloomers in her day. Whatever, we've got 'em.

How did Queen Victoria's bloomers end up at the **Kent State University Fashion Museum** (Rockwell Hall, Kent State University, Kent; 330-672-3450)? They were part of a collection of 13 pieces of royal underwear and linens purchased by museum founders Shannon Rodgers and Jerry Silverman, probably at an auction in England.

Sadly for you voyeurs out there, the Queen's underwear is not on

display at present. Museum staff said it is "resting," whatever that means. But it may be back on display in the future. And meanwhile you can see lots of other underwear (and outerwear) from all over the world. The collection contains more than 20,000 historic and contemporary world costumes.

Now Hear This:

KENT

A casual remark during a interview with *National Hearing Aid Journal* was all it took to start the donations pouring in to Professor Kenneth Berger at Kent State University. Now that university has the largest collection of hearing aids in the world, housed in the **Kenneth W. Berger Hearing Aid Museum and Archives** (Music and Speech Building, Kent State University, Kent).

More than 3,000 different models of hearing aid are collected in large wooden cases in the hallway of the Speech Pathology and

BIG MOUSETRAP

LISBON

They say if you build a better mousetrap the world will beat a path to your door.

If that's the case, there must be a four-lane highway leading to the door of the Columbiana Career Center in Lisbon.

The students there set out to build the largest working model of the world's most popular mousetrap. And they did set a world's record in the Guinness book with a Victor-style mousetrap that was 9 feet, 10 inches long and 4 feet, 5 inches wide. And it actually works! If you were strong enough to hold back the spring, you could probably catch a bear in this baby.

The project was designed for the students to not only learn but to make some money for the student fund. The trap used to be on display at the school but has now been sold to a museum in Florida, and memories and a few pictures are all that is left at the school.

Audiology Clinic. The devices range from cumbersome vacuum-tube affairs to modern digital models. Many are demonstrated on mannequin heads (stylishly outfitted with period hats and scarves). One of the earliest exhibits is a 160-year-old silver ear trumpet from England. There are several examples of eyeglass hearing aids, which became popular when Eleanor Roosevelt was photographed using one.

The museum has been around since 1966, but it doesn't promote itself much. It is open for tours.

The Non-Electric Store

KIDRON

Lehman's Hardware (One Lehman Circle, Kidron; 877-438-5346) claims to be the only "non-electric" hardware store in Ohio.

Located in the midst of Ohio's Amish country, the store has al-

ways carried the things the Amish use in their simple non-electric lifestyle. You can still buy a wood-burning cook stove here, brand new. You can also find things like oil lamps and lanterns, wringers, and hand-operated washing machines. You can even find a non-electric freezer here, powered by kerosene. It's like wandering through a general store from your great-grandmother's time.

Lehman's was a popular place during the Y2K scare at the end of 1999. City folks who thought they were going to lose their light and heat started a buying frenzy here, stocking up on wood-fired stoves, gasoline-powered washing machines, and the like. (Lehman's was more than a year behind in orders for the cook stoves at the height of the panic.) The Amish, who live this way all the time, just smiled and perhaps chuckled a bit at the actions of their panicky "Yankee" neighbors.

The Mailbox Factory

KIRTLAND

Wayne Burwell is a man who knows how to take a lemon and make lemonade out of it. He used to make his living plowing snow in the area around Kirtland, the heart of Ohio's snowbelt. Once in a while his plow would knock over a mailbox. As part of his service, Burwell would rebuild and replace the mailbox.

His work was so good that some folks started approaching him to build mailboxes for them *before* he knocked over their old ones. Then one day a customer asked Wayne if he could make the mailbox look like his earthmover. Wayne did, and a new business was born.

Today he heads up the **Mailbox Factory** (7857 Chardon Rd., Kirt-land; 888-740-6245), and his mailboxes are unusual creations. One looks like a giant tooth being held up by a giant toothbrush. One's a replica of my 1959 Nash Metropolitan.

The Giant Easter Basket

LORAIN

Lorain's most notable landmark may be the giant Easter basket.

Lakeview Park, on West Erie Avenue, was laid out as a public works project in 1937, with a fountain in the middle of the rose garden (the lights changed color at night) and one of the best swimming beaches along Lake Erie.

Proud park officials wanted a fancy entrance at the end of the driveway. "Make something special," they told parks department mechanic David Shukait. He did.

He took some boards and built a long, curving form. He mixed up some concrete and started filling the molds. When he was done, he had dozens of what looked like giant stone bands, which he started assembling like a jigsaw puzzle.

And then it took shape: a huge concrete basket, 10 feet wide and nearly 9 feet high. Shukait painted it up to look like a gaily decorated flower basket, and because Easter was just around the corner but it was too early for flowers, he made nearly a dozen two-foot long concrete eggs and placed them in the basket. A tradition was born.

Nearly every Easter since, Lorain families have come to pay homage to the giant Easter basket and have their picture taken in front of it.

There were some problems. In the early years, teenagers got into the habit of swiping the eggs, which weighed nearly a hundred pounds each, sometimes having impromptu contests to see who could throw one the farthest.

So park officials redesigned the eggs, making them lighter, and now they are placed in the basket only during the week between Palm Sunday and Easter Sunday.

Now, I ask you, what's better than having a giant Easter basket? Having two, of course. Shukait actually made another, which is located at **Oakwood Park**, on Grove Avenue.

Longest Bascule Bridge in the U.S.

LORAIN

When you drive across the **Charles Berry Memorial Bascule Bridge**, over the Black River in Lorain, you're driving over the longest bascule, or lift, bridge in the United States and the second-largest in the world.

Built in 1940, it stretches 333 feet across the mouth of the river in front of what was once the Lorain Shipyards (owned by New York Yankees owner George Steinbrenner).

The bridge surface is a grid that you can see through when driving over it; an operator at the edge of the river can raise the two halves into an upright position when a large boat or tall sailboat wants to enter or exit the river.

The bridge, which is located on East Erie Avenue just east of

Broadway in downtown Lorain, was named for Lorain native Corporal Charles Berry, USMC, who was posthumously awarded the Medal of Honor in World War II.

Easter Bunny's Helper

LYNDHURST

In 1957 Ron and Betty Manolio of Lyndhurst decided to celebrate Easter by creating a mosaic in their front yard. It depicted a cross and an Easter bunny, and it was made from 750 colored Easter eggs. The shells were emptied before painting, so many were able to be preserved for the next year. Each subsequent year, the Manolios added more and more and more eggs. The total now exceeds fifty thousand! The scenes change every year (with the exception of the cross and the Easter Bunny) and often include popular characters such as the Flintstones and the Jetsons. Each year the display attracts many visitors and plenty of attention from both local and national media. **Egg Shell Land** (1031 Linden Ln., Lyndhurst) continues despite occasional disasters, such as a hailstorm one Easter that broke more than ten thousand eggs, and six inches of snow another year that covered up the display.

A Hollywood Wedding in Mansfield

MANSFIELD

Humphrey Bogart and Lauren Bacall were married in Ohio. On May 21, 1945, the Hollywood lovebirds tied the knot at Malabar Farm near Mansfield, then owned by Bogart's friend, Louis Bromfield.

Bogart was visiting Bromfield when the urge to marry struck. Bacall arrived in Mansfield by train. They went to the farm in a swirl of publicity and were planning to be married in the garden, but the number of curious onlookers forced them to hold the ceremony inside on the stairway to the second floor.

That evening, following the wedding, Bromfield showed them to the house's "honeymoon suite," a bedroom at the top of the stairs with two twin-sized beds in it.

Bogie and Bacall trod these stairs on their way to the "honeymoon suite" with twin beds.

Today the farm is a state park, and the home is very much as it was in the 1940s, including the Bogart-Bacall wedding suite. Tour guides note that both the twin beds had wheels on them, so they could easily be pushed together.

Malabar Farm State Park (4050 Bromfield Rd., Lucas; 419-892-2784) is open to the public year 'round.

One of Johnny Appleseed's Original Trees

MANSFIELD

This place is a real mixed bag. It's perhaps the oldest veterans meeting hall in the country. It's a former zoo. It's an unusual museum. And it's haunted.

The Mansfield Memorial Museum (34 Park Ave. W., Mansfield; 419-525-2491) opened its doors back in 1889. Veterans who fought at Gettysburg and Shiloh met in these rooms, as did those who charged up San Juan Hill during the Spanish-American War. Next came the vets who fought in France in World War I, and so on. Now veterans of Vietnam and the Gulf War use the same chairs that Civil War veterans did to hold their meetings.

The building was also the first zoo in Mansfield. They kept live exotic animals, like monkeys and rheas, in cages on the third floor. The zoo closed when the animals died, so they mounted them—and you can still see some of them today.

As for the ghost, the present curator reports that he has heard footsteps on the upper floors, and he says that when he displayed a picture of the first curator (whom he believes to be the ghost) the subject was frowning, but when he came back the next day, the man appeared to be smiling.

The museum was reopened a few years ago with the original 1889 display cases and a wild and wonderful collection befitting a museum from the Gay '90s.

Besides uniforms and swords from all the wars mentioned above there are the collections of stuffed birds (some now extinct), fish, and butterflies; native American artifacts; pieces of wood from Oliver Hazard Perry's flagship the *Lawrence*; a handmade pike used by John Brown in his Harpers Ferry raid; and a Victorian assembly of stuffed animals dressed up in clothes and shown taking part in human activities. They even have an apple tree that was originally planted by the legendary Johnny Appleseed. The whole tree!

Open weekends, and by appointment at other times.

This family of deceased ducks dressed for dinner in their cozy glass case at Mansfield Memorial Museum.

Reformatory with a Gift Shop

MANSFIELD

Mansfield is home to one spooky-looking tourist attraction—the former Ohio State Reformatory. Built in 1886, this huge castle-like structure takes up more than 175,000 square feet and combines four architectural styles: Victorian, Gothic, Romanesque, and Queen Anne. It also houses the world's tallest freestanding steel cell block. It has six tiers and 12 ranges with more than 550 cells.

The prison operated until 1990, when it was finally closed, and a new prison opened about a mile away.

A local nonprofit historical society was formed to preserve the old prison, but before they could act the state started demolition, taking down the brooding walls that surrounded the main building.

The society was able to save the rest of the structure and is now working to raise funds to restore it. In the meantime, Hollywood has discovered the old lockup; it has been used in several movies, including *The Shawshank Redemption*, *Air Force One*, and *Tango and Cash*, and on such TV shows as Fox's *Scariest Places on Earth*. A visit to the Mansfield reformatory was included in the Travel Channel's list of "101 Things to Do Before You Die."

The **Ohio State Reformatory Historic Site** (100 Reformatory Rd., Mansfield; 419-522-2644) is now open for tours (including *The Dungeon Tour* and *The Hollywood Tour*) on Sundays starting the week after Mother's Day through the end of September. Some of the guides are former guards, and the visitors have included former inmates who have returned, sometimes with family, to look at the place where they spent a chunk of their lives. The tour includes places where the movies were shot. Guides point out that Gates Brown, a baseball player with the Detroit Tigers, served a term here for burglary in the 1950s, and Cleveland Browns star running back Kevin Mack once spent a month here on a drug charge.

The Mansfield Reformatory Gift Shop sells movie memorabilia, hats, T-shirts, and keychains, and also some crafts made by present-day prisoners down the road at the new prison.

A Biblical Wax Museum

MANSFIELD

The only real wax museum in Ohio is in Mansfield: the **Living Bible Museum and Bible Walk** (500 Tingley Ave., Mansfield; 419-524-0139). A tribute to the Bible, it re-creates 70 dramatic life-size scenes from both the Old and New Testaments. Some of the over 300 wax figures are hand-me-downs from other museums that were repurposed by the Mansfield organization. So, if you look closely, you'll notice that some of the biblical figures bear a striking resemblance to Hollywood stars and other famous people. Elizabeth Taylor, for example, appears in the scene telling the story of Solomon.

One Store, Two States

MASURY

The **Penn-Ohio Medicine Mart** (850 S. Irvine Ave, Masury) really crosses the line. Literally. Part of the store is Pennsylvania and part of it is in Ohio.

When they sell lottery tickets they have to have two machines, one for each state—and by law the machines have to be located in the state that issues the tickets. So management drew a line through the store; as you shop, you cross back and forth from one state to the other—soft drinks in Ohio, prescriptions filled in Pennsylvania.

The store even has two mailing addresses: 830 South Irvine Avenue, Sharon, Pennsylvania, and 830 South Irvine Avenue, Masury, Ohio. The phone numbers are also different. If you are in Pennsylvania and you want to call the Penn-Ohio Medicine Mart, the number is 724-347-5505; Ohioans dial 330-448-0770.

When asked if dealing with laws in two states and having two addresses and phone numbers was confusing, a clerk just smiled and said, "You get used to it." But she said it does get hectic when one of the two state lotteries reaches an unusually high amount. "Then we have lines that literally spill from one state to the next."

A Sundae with Everything–Including the Kitchen Sink

MEDINA

Ohio has two ice-cream museums. One is operated by the Velvet Ice Cream Company in Utica.

The other is in Medina, at Elm Farms, once one of the larger dairies in northern Ohio.

Carl Abell had actually been out of the business for a few years when he started making ice cream again to go along with an ice-cream museum he installed in his former dairy.

What makes his operation unusual is a sundae that they serve called "The Kitchen Sink." It's literally served in a stainless-steel sink. The sundae, which costs in the neighborhood of $40, contains

at least 21 dips of different premium ice-cream flavors, topped with a rainbow of syrups, toppings, and whipped cream.

Unlike some of the other giant-size servings offered by promotion-minded restaurateurs, this one you pay for even if you manage to eat the whole thing.

The **Elm Farms Dairy and Once Upon a Sundae Ice Cream Parlor** are located at 1050 West Lafayette Road, Medina; 330-722-3839.

THE DAY THE SKY FELL

NEW CONCORD

On May 1, 1860, the folks in New Concord must have thought the sky was really falling.

Residents reported hearing a humongous roar that lasted nearly a minute. It was near high noon on a clear day, and across the heavens a meteorite had entered the earth's atmosphere and was headed straight for the tiny community. As it hit the dense atmosphere it started breaking up, leaving a trail of fireworks across the sky and in all likelihood frightening the bejesus out of people and animals.

The only casualty occurred when one piece of the meteorite slammed into a cow, killing it instantly. Folks all over the county were later picking up bits of the meteorite—more than 500 pounds of space rock in all (and scientists say they probably missed much more that buried itself in the ground of Muskingum County). One of the largest chunks of meteorite recovered weighed more than 100 pounds; it is now owned by the geology department of Marietta College.

The only casualty occurred when one piece of the meteorite slammed into a cow.

The Bridge to Nowhere

MENTOR

There is a bridge in Mentor that starts no place and goes nowhere (**Mentor Lagoons Nature Preserve and Marina**, 8365 Harbor Dr., Mentor; 440-974-5720).

Back in the 1920s when the lagoons next to the huge Mentor Marsh were first being developed, entrepreneurs decided Mentor was going to be the "Venice of the North." There would be canals with beautiful homes lining the tree-shaded waterways. And the entryway to all of this development was going to be a magnificent bridge connecting Lake Shore Boulevard with the lagoons. Not in the developers' plan, though, was the stock market crash of 1929. After that, the Mentor lagoon project foundered and was financially abandoned.

Some things take on a life of their own, though, when government is involved. The bridge that was to be the dramatic entrance to the Venice of the North had been planned, and local government had slowly been grinding out the necessary permits and zoning approvals. In 1932, even though the dream of a waterway community was in bankruptcy, the city went ahead and built the bridge. Now, the actual road connecting to Lake Shore Boulevard had not been built, of course. Still, a huge concrete bridge went up over the first lagoon—connected to nothing, just a field. You can see it today as you float down the lagoons. Its crumbling concrete has weathered more than 70 years, and there have been periodic calls for its demolition by boaters. Both ends of the bridge have been closed to stop daredevil youngsters who used the bridge to dive into the shallow lagoon below. It might be considered a monument to looking before you leap.

The entryway to all of this development was going to be a magnificent bridge connecting Lake Shore Boulevard with the lagoons.

World's Largest Horse and Buggy

MESOPOTAMIA

What is perhaps one of the strangest statues in Ohio stands at the center of the tiny Amish community of Mesopotamia, in Trumbull County.

It's a wooden statue of a giant horse and buggy.

The statue is 32 feet long and 14 feet high. The buggy wheels are each over 7 feet high.

It was the idea and the project of the Schaden family, which operates the nearby End of the Commons General Store in Mesopotamia.

A local artist, Chris McConnell, created the giant horse and buggy using 2,300 feet of lumber, including seasoned two-by-fours. It is held together by 30 pounds of wooden screws.

A sign in front of the statue, for Amish visitors, I guess, gives the height of the sculpture in horse measurements. It's approximately 29 hands high.

The biggest horse and buggy can be found at the corner of state routes 87 and 534 in Mesopotamia. Be sure to bring along your camera.

A Horse and Buggy Stop Sign

MIDDLEFIELD

When we see an octagonal red sign at an intersection, we expect it to read "STOP." But in Middlefield, home to the second-largest Amish population in Ohio, one warning sign says not "STOP" but "WHOA." I guess that's appropriate for all the horse-and-buggy traffic in the area. You can see the "WHOA" sign at the intersection of the parking lot and the highway at **Mary Yoder's Amish Kitchen Restaurant** (14743 N. State St., Middlefield; 440-632-1939) in Geauga County. I'm not quite certain that horses can read, so if you see a horse and buggy coming out of the parking lot, be careful.

The Inventor of the Electric Chair

MILAN

Thomas Edison, not wanting himself associated with capital punishment, went to great lengths to make sure the world's first electric chair was powered by his biggest competitor, George Westinghouse.

Another Ohioan, Dr. Alphonso David Rockwell (who also hailed from Edison's hometown of Milan) was a more willing participant.

Rockwell was noted for his research into medical uses for electricity and was selected for a committee of five persons directed to design and build the world's first electric chair for Auburn Prison in New York. He seemed to relish the challenge, and he drew up the plans for the first chair, which took the life of convicted murderer William Kemmler, alias John Hart, on August 6, 1890. He also wrote about it in his autobiography, *Rambling Recollection*, which was published in 1920. (Edison didn't even mention the chair in his own book.)

The Street with No Name

MILLERSBURG

Most streets and roads have names. Some describe the route between cities, like Milan-Elyria Telegraph Road. Some grant a bit of immortality to a person or family, like Becker Road or Smith Road. Sometimes a manufacturer gets into the act: in Cleveland, an alley near a commercial bakery was renamed Twinkie Lane for the dessert cake they made. But the good folks down in Millersburg, where they still have hitching rails for horses in the downtown area, took an unusual approach to naming one city street. The new street, which crossed Monroe Street on the south side of town, was originally listed as having no name. Because you need street names for maps, they corrected the situation. The name they chose? No Name Street.

The Last Sword Maker in America

NEW LONDON

It's no secret why swords don't sell all that well anymore. They haven't been used in battle since the Civil War. There just isn't much demand now for a four-foot blade.

But in New London, tiny **Ames Sword Company** (S. Railroad St., New London; 800-345-3682) keeps the sword-making tradition alive.

The company started out in 1791 in Chelmsford, Massachusetts. In 1832 they signed their first contract with the U.S. government to make swords for artillerymen. After that, Ames swords were carried in just about every famous military battle that the U.S. fought. Privates and presidents have carried and owned Ames swords. The first presentation swords ever commissioned by the government, to honor heroes of the Mexican War in the early 1800s, were made by Ames.

The business was sold during the Great Depression to a Columbus firm, and again in 1951 to C. E. Ward Company of New London.

Surprisingly, swords are still made much as they were two hundred years ago, one at a time, by hand. Who buys them? Fraternal organizations, like the Masons and Knights of Columbus, account for a large portion of the number made each year. The U.S. armed forces still use them for ceremonial purposes.

Sadly, after I mentioned this company in one of my books, they were inundated by people who wanted to take tours of the factory. There had been a longstanding, informal understanding that if someone dropped in at the factory and wanted to look around, and an employee could be found who was not too busy, a tour would quickly be arranged. That came to a screeching halt when they started spending a good part of the day doing tours and not getting any work done. You're still invited to stop in at the factory and browse through their store, where you can see samples of the various swords they sell. (You are invited to buy a sword, too, if you are in the market.) But don't ask for a tour. They say they are just too busy.

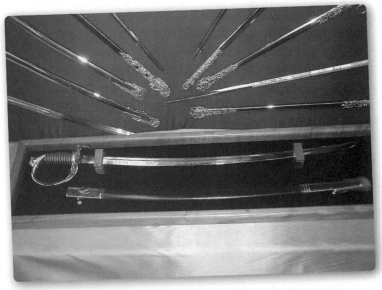

Sasquatch Hunter
NEWCOMERSTOWN

Don Keating of Newcomerstown has devoted about half of his life to research on sightings of Sasquatch, or "Bigfoot."

Although Sasquatch sightings are more common in the northwestern U.S., Don says there have been sightings in nearly every state in the union. In Ohio alone, there are about a hundred sightings a year.

Keating himself has never seen a real Sasquatch, but, he quickly adds, that doesn't mean they don't exist.

The reason he says this is a set of plaster casts he made in 1990 in Tuscarawas County. Don had received word of a Bigfoot sighting along Big Lick Road, just outside of Newcomerstown. He searched there for evidence but found none. Over the next year he occasionally checked the same area, and one day as he was driving down the road he spotted, on a muddy stretch alongside the road, three huge, widely spaced, footprints. Each was 17 inches long and nearly 11 inches wide at the toe spread. Their depth mud indicated a very heavy animal or object. The spread of the footprints suggested they must have been made by something with a stride of four to six feet.

Keating has shown the casts to hunters and other outdoors experts, but no one has been able to say exactly what could have made the footprints.

What did he find? Keating isn't sure, but he doesn't rule out the footprints of an Ohio Sasquatch. He holds annual meetings in Newcomerstown for other researchers into Sasquatch phenomena.

Ride Till You Hurl:
The New Philadelphia Carousel

NEW PHILADELPHIA

There's a graceful 36-seat, all-wood antique carousel in New Philadelphia that local families have ridden for four or five generations.
And there's something special about this particular carousel. The
operators let you ride till you almost toss your cookies.

This may be the longest carousel ride in existence. They don't
use a timer and just let the thing go, round and round, until the
operator notices a kid getting a bit green or starting to look franti-
cally around for Mom or Dad. To be honest, that really doesn't happen so often. Most kids love it. It's like getting on the ride and having the operator forget you're on board.

Here's the next good part. The cost of the ride is just 50 cents.

The Herschell-Spillman carousel, built in 1928 in North
Tonawanda, New York, was purchased second hand in 1940 by the
city fathers of New Philadelphia. They wanted a special attraction
for **Tuscora Park** (161 Tuscora Ave., New Philadelphia; 330-343-6814),
the city playground. Today there are a half-dozen other kiddy rides,
as well as a Ferris wheel, a huge swimming pool, and a youth center.

This Museum Officially Sucks

NORTH CANTON

In 1910, the new Kotten suction cleaner required the user to stand
on a platform and rock back and forth. The rocking action activated
a bellows under the platform that created the suction to clean with.
It gave the operator quite a workout and was very slow in cleaning.
But considering the alternative at the time—hauling the carpet out
to a clothesline and then beating it with a stick—it probably seemed
like a really neat invention.

The **Hoover Historical Center** (1875 Easton St. NW, North Canton;

330-499-0287) has the Kotten on display. Today Ohio lays claim to the only vacuum cleaner museum in the nation. Here you can also see the first cleaning machine sold by Hoover way back in 1908; it weighed almost 40 pounds! Carry that one up and down the stairs a few times. They also have a Hoover cleaner called a Constellation that was a big hit in the 1950s. When you turn it on, it floats on a cushion of air. There were no wheels, so it could easily follow you wherever you went.

You can also find some interesting items used by housewives years before suction cleaners were invented.

Here's an invention you can't beat with a stick!

Harry Stevens and the Hot Dog
NILES

The next time you hear the phrase "As American as baseball, hot dogs, apple pie, and ice cream," think of Harry Stevens. The Niles native created the American hot dog as we know it today.

Stevens operated concessions at several big sporting complexes around the turn of the twentieth century. He sold things like scorecards, hard-boiled eggs, beer, and popcorn at games.

One very cold day in 1901 at a New York Giants game at the old polo grounds, ice cream and cold beer were just not selling. Harry had an inspiration. He sent his workers into the surrounding neighborhood to buy out all the little sausages, called "dachshund sausages," and Vienna rolls. Back at the ball yard they quickly boiled the sausages in a large vat of water, sliced open the rolls, plunked the puffed-up wieners between the bread halves, and slathered on some mustard. Then, for the first time in history, fans heard the cry, "Get yer redhots here! Get 'em while they're hot!"

The hot sandwiches were an instant hit.

In the crowd that fateful day was sports cartoonist Thomas Aloysius Dorgan. He noticed the new sandwich being sold and drew a cartoon. It featured four-legged frankfurters and the patrons reaching for them. Dorgan couldn't remember how to spell "dachshund," so in the caption he just wrote "hot dog." The rest, as they say, is history.

Stevens never forgot his Ohio roots. Despite his successes in the concessions biz, he and his wife Mary and their kids always lived in Niles, and today there is a city park in Niles that honors Harry Stevens, the father of the "hot dog."

A New Use for Covered Bridges

NORTH KINGSVILLE

What do you do with a covered bridge you no longer need? Ashtabula County put one of theirs up for sale in the early 1970s with the stipulation that the buyer had to move it. A local entrepreneur bought the bridge, sawed it in two, and moved one half to North Kingsville and the other to Andover . . . to become pizza restaurants. Today you can grab a cheese and pepperoni pie while gazing at the initials and graffiti carved into the timbers of the old bridge a century or more ago at the original **Covered Bridge Pizza** (6541 S. Main St., North Kingsville; 440-224-2252).

Ohio's First Traffic Fatality

NORWICH

Christopher Columbus Baldwin secured a place in American history. Two places, actually. That second chance at fame, though, he might have preferred to miss.

Baldwin was the second librarian of the American Antiquarian Society, a group that built and still maintains a national library of American history literature and culture. He served from 1827 to

Speed was blamed in Ohio's first recorded traffic fatality, when a stagecoach rolled over near this spot.

1835 and was personally responsible for obtaining thousands of works for the library from early American authors and publishers.

It was in the pursuit of this work that Baldwin gained a second kind of fame: Christopher Columbus Baldwin became **Ohio's first known traffic fatality**.

In 1835 the American Antiquarian Society, headquartered in Massachusetts, ordered Baldwin to head out to the Ohio frontier to investigate some recently discovered ancient American Indian burial mounds in southern Ohio.

There weren't many ways to travel to Ohio in those days. Either you went by riverboat from Pittsburgh down the Ohio River or by boat from Buffalo on Lake Erie to one of the Ohio ports, like Cleveland, or you took your chances on the National Road, which stretched from the east coast to the Mississippi Valley. The National Road, built by the federal government during Thomas Jefferson's presidency, was in some places a road in name only.

An author named Charles Fenno Hoffman described his ride on the National Road in 1833 this way: "The ruts are worn so broad and deep by heavy travel that an army of pygmies might march into the bosom of the country under the cover they provide!"

It was on the National Road (today U.S. 40), that Christopher Columbus Baldwin chose to make his trek, by stagecoach, to southern Ohio.

On August 20, 1835, while speeding down a winding hill into the village of Norwich, the stagecoach ran off the road at a curve and rolled over. When rescuers reached the wreckage of the coach, they found the 35-year-old Baldwin inside, dead.

A stone and bronze tablet, perhaps the only monument to commemorate a traffic accident, was erected at the site in 1925 by the Norwich Boy Scout Troop, commemorating the man who became the Buckeye State's first traffic fatality.

The memorial stone is located on old U.S. Route 40 at the eastern end of the village of Norwich, on the north side of the road at a sharp curve.

The Tracks to the Underground

OBERLIN

You're driving along Professor Street in Oberlin, and suddenly, across from the Conservatory of Music, you see a strange sight: a pair of railroad tracks rising into the air. It looks like the tracks sprouted from some collapsed underground railroad. The first time I saw it, I thought it was a college prank.

Turns out, it's a piece of outdoor sculpture and a symbol of the role Oberlin and Oberlin College played in the Underground Railroad before the Civil War.

Oberlin was a strong abolitionist community, firmly against slavery. In fact, it has been called "the little town that started the Civil War." The Underground Railroad was a series of homes and buildings across the northern states during the early 19th century that sheltered escaped slaves and helped them make their way to freedom in Canada.

In 1977, Oberlin College architectural student Cameron Armstrong, class of '77, designed the railroad tracks coming out of the ground. It was only meant to be a temporary project, but its popu-

THE BUDGET

SUGARCREEK

> **"Joseph Yoder had a big explosion, but it turned out to just be a strawberry can. It flew all the way up to the ceiling and made quite a mess."**

That's the kind of news story you're likely to read in *The Budget*, the small Sugarcreek newspaper published for Amish and Mennonite readers locally and throughout the world.

The reporters, or "scribes," as they are called, are members of the Amish and Mennonite communities, and their "stories" are in the form of long letters that they write to the editor of the newspaper, who then publishes them pretty much as they are written.

It may seem quaint to some, but *The Budget* sells big time, not only to the Amish and Mennonites, but also to many other people around the world who enjoy reading about the simple lifestyle of the "plain people," and enjoy the sometimes unintentional humor of their writing: "Dennis Miller started out to plow this morning and came across a soft place when all at once the horse went down and all that would have been needed would be a few shovels of dirt and he would have been covered up."

Then there's the way they can often look on the bright side, even when reporting a serious accident: "David L. Yoder had quite an experience late Monday, when he got gas on his clothes, which caught fire. He buried himself in hay and smothered the flames. It is a great wonder that the hay didn't start to burn. He got a few burns on his neck and lost some hair and whiskers, but his clothes aren't damaged much."

The Budget is now in its second century, and little has changed since it began publication in 1890.

larity has made it a permanent fixture. You can see it today in front of Talcott Hall on South Professor Street near the intersection of West College Street.

Squeeze Box Heaven

ROCKY RIVER

Ohio has an official state rock song, "Hang on Sloopy." We honor the ladybug as our official state insect. Tomato juice is our official state drink. If we were to have an official musical instrument, it probably ought to be the accordion. Jack and Kathy White would agree. They turned the basement of their suburban Cleveland home into a museum dedicated to the instrument. It holds more than 300 accordions and also sheet music, pictures of famous accordion players, and accordion memorabilia.

Visitors here learn that accordions are not just for polka bands; they have even been used in symphony orchestras. Although keyboards and computerized instruments have largely pushed them aside in recent years, Jack and Kathy White think nothing else sounds like the real thing, and at the drop of a hat Jack will strap one on and play a tune.

The **Cleveland Accordion Museum** (18974 Story Rd., Rocky River; 440-895-9223) is open only by appointment. Call first to make sure someone is at home.

The Giants of Seville

SEVILLE

Once, giants walked among us. At least they did in the Medina County farming village of Seville.

In the Mound Hill Cemetery in Seville, there is a tall stone statue of a woman. Some say it is supposed to be a likeness of Anna Swan Bates. It stands over the graves of Anna and her husband, Martin Bates, once known worldwide as the "World's Tallest Married Couple."

Bates, who stood just a hair under eight feet tall, had been a Confederate soldier in the Civil War. His wife, Anna Swan Bates, who was about an inch or two taller than her husband, was born in Nova Scotia and had been discovered by P. T. Barnum. The two met when Bates went to work for Barnum after the Civil War, and they eventually married. They toured the world, appearing before the crowned heads of Europe.

A couple of circus friends happened to own farms in Seville, and during the off-season the Bateses visited their friends and enjoyed the small town and its rural countryside so much they also decided to buy a farm and make Seville their home.

It was while living in Seville that Anna Bates became pregnant and, after a difficult delivery on January 18, 1879, gave birth to a giant baby boy—30 inches long and 23½ pounds at birth. Each of his feet was six inches long. Sadly, he only lived 11 hours. He, too, is buried in the Mound Hill Cemetery.

Captain Bates had his farm home custom built. The ceilings were 14 feet high, all the doors were 8½ feet tall, even the cellar was more

Captain Martin Bates was one half of the world's tallest married couples when he was married to Anna Swan Bates.

than 9 feet deep. The specially built furniture was so massive that when average-sized guests visited, the women would usually stand rather than suffer the indignity of having to be hoisted up onto the seat. In those pre-automobile days, the Bateses had a specially built carriage that was pulled by two giant Clydesdale workhorses. After being forced to stand during a service at the local Baptist church because they were too tall to fit in the regular-sized church pews, Bates had a special large pew made just for his family, so they could sit during the service.

On August 5, 1888, Anna Swan Bates died of kidney failure. She was just 42 years old. Captain Bates telegraphed a casket company in Cleveland to send a casket to hold the remains of a person eight feet tall. The casket company, thinking the size was a misprint, sent a normal-sized casket. Bates went into a fury over the mistake, and they had to delay the funeral three days until the special casket could be constructed and shipped to Seville.

Following his wife's funeral, Bates, taking no chances on a repeat of the casket fiasco, ordered a second extra-long casket for himself and stored it in his barn for years until it was finally needed.

Bates was lonely after the death of Anna and a few years later married Annette Weatherby, the five-foot-tall daughter of his pastor. He also gave up the giant house on the farm and moved into a normal-sized home in downtown Seville. (He did enlarge the bedroom to hold his 10-foot-long bed, and he brought with him some of his favorite chairs.)

From all accounts the tall captain had a short temper, and old age did not improve his disposition. He took to chewing tobacco in his later years and was known to spit at people he did not like. His investments and the income from his farm allowed him to live out his life comfortably in the little northern Ohio town. He died at the age of 74 in January 1919.

A few old-timers in Seville still remember Captain Bates. Many of the places associated with his life still stand. The **Seville Historical Society** (70 W. Main St., Seville; 330-769-4056) has some of his clothing and life-size pictures of him and his first wife, Anna Swan Bates, that visitors can pose with. The farm home is gone, but the barn still remains.

In the Mound Hill Cemetery, the statue to Anna Bates now stands eternal guard over the graves of Martin, Anna, and their baby.

The Second-Oldest Drive-In Movie Theater in the U.S.

STRASBURG

Lynn Drive-In Movies (9735 State Rte. 250 NW, Strasburg; 330-878-5797) in Strasburg has the honor of being the second-oldest continuously operating drive-in movie theater in the nation (the oldest—built in 1934—is in Orefield, Pennsylvania) and the oldest in Ohio.

Construction started in 1935, and the Strasburg theater, first known as Boyer's Auto Theater, welcomed its first automobiles in the spring of 1937. The name was changed to Lynn Auto Theater in 1948 when it was sold and one of the new owners, Ray McCombs, decided to rename it in honor of his daughter, Judy Lynn. It changed owners again in the 1950s, but the new owners, who still operate the theater, decided to leave the name alone.

Today the theater has two screens with wireless HD stereo sound and a "Classic Mammoth Retro Neon Marquee." Even in this age of computers and DVD movies, the old Lynn Drive-In Movies still attracts crowds on a summer night.

Lions and Tigers and Bears and Bed-and-Breakfast

SUGARCREEK

The Bed and Breakfast Barn (560 Sugarcreek St., Sugarcreek; 330-852-2337) is a rustic country inn with the usual amenities—and a basement full of animals.

The basement contains the White Fawn Wildlife Exhibit—more than 300 mounted animals ranging from cougars to deer to a host of other North American wildlife. You can see black bears stalking trout, wild turkeys about to take flight at the approach of mountain lions, and many other animals, all mounted in settings that make them look almost like they did in life. You don't even have to spend

the night at the bed-and-breakfast. For $1 per person they offer tours of the exhibit to anyone who drops in.

Now before you get excited and start writing letters, Tom Agler, the owner, didn't kill any of these animals. He purchased them from collectors and at disposal sales held by law-enforcement organizations that had confiscated them originally from poachers and other individuals who had obtained them illegally.

If you prefer your animals alive, the Bed and Breakfast Barn also has a petting zoo with deer, goats, donkeys, llamas, rabbits, chickens, ducks, and two bears.

The Sign of the Three Crosses

SUGARCREEK

If you travel rural Ohio you may have seen them. Three crosses: two blue and one yellow. No signs, no banners, just three simple wooden crosses, usually standing beside a rural road.

The man responsible for them was Bernie Coffindaffer. A self-made millionaire from West Virginia, Coffindaffer was told by Jesus, in a 1983 vision, to go around the country putting up the crosses. And Jesus told him just what the crosses should look like.

Coffindaffer sold his business and spent the rest of his life finding locations, getting permission, and building crosses. By 1993, when he died, he had 1,800 sets of three crosses in 29 states and in the Philippines. Friends said that he spent over three million dollars in his pilgrimage, all of his savings, to complete his mission.

There are 89 locations in Ohio where Bernie Coffindaffer placed crosses. But now, years after his death, maintenance on most of the crosses has ceased. Some have fallen down or been taken down by property owners. In a few cases they have been kept standing as a silent tribute to one man's faith in his God.

One set of crosses in particularly good condition is on Ohio Route 39, on the east side of Sugarcreek.

Have a Ball in Tiro

EVENTS!

TIRO

It's really just a wide spot in the road with three or four businesses, but each April thousands of people travel to Tiro from several states to take part in a most unusual festival. What they celebrate at that festival is the part of a bull that makes a bull a bull. Yep, some people call them "mountain oysters" or "prairie oysters," but these oysters have never seen the sea.

It started simply back in the 1990s, when the owner of the Tiro Tavern was given a box of the delicacies. He fried them up and handed them out to his patrons. Since then it's become a tradition one weekend in April each year, and they now cook upwards of a half ton of the gonads to satisfy the growing crowds. There is no parade, no queen selected, no rides—so what is there to do at this festival? As one woman told me: "We drink beer and eat testicles." And that is precisely what they do at the **Tiro Testicle Festival** (102 S. Main Street, Tiro; 419-347-6922). Everyone really has a ball.

World's Largest Gathering of Twins
TWINSBURG

EVENTS!

Would the world's largest gathering of twins be as exciting in a town called Millsville? Probably not. Luckily, Moses and Aaron Wilcox had their way back in 1819.

When the Wilcox brothers, who were twins, moved to what was then known as Millsville, they offered the tiny community six acres of land for a public square in the village, and $20 toward the start of a school, if the community would agree to change the name to Twinsburg.

The townspeople complied but didn't decide to celebrate the name until a festival honoring twins was organized in 1976. Only 37 sets of twins, mostly from northern Ohio, showed up for that first one-day event. They dedicated a monument to the Wilcox brothers and partook in the usual small-town festival events.

Since then, **Twins Days** (330-425-3652) has grown into a two-day international festival attracting nearly 3,000 sets of twins each year from as far away as Poland and Nigeria. (Other "multiples"—triplets, quads, and even quintuplets—participate.) The festival draws coverage from news media all over the world. It is held the first full weekend in August.

The festival is now listed in the *Guinness Book of World Records* as the largest gathering of twins in the world. They have featured a double wedding of two sets of twins, and efforts are underway to build a Twins Hall of Fame in the community.

The Town Where They Race Worms

EVENTS!

VERMILION

Vermilion may be the only place on earth where thousands of people come together each autumn to watch worms race.

The event was conceived of by Dick Goddard, one of the most widely respected weathermen in the U.S. (and my former colleague at Fox 8 TV).

Woollybears are those little furry worms we see in late summer and early fall. They have fuzzy coats of brown and orange. Weather folklore claims that the severity of the coming winter can be predicted by the woollybear caterpillars' fuzzy coats—something about the length of the brown part, or it is the orange?

The **Woollybear Festival** started as a PTA fundraiser in Birmingham in 1973 and has grown into the largest single-day festival in Ohio, attracting upward of 150,000 people to the small town of Vermilion (where it was moved after the first couple of years to better accommodate the crowd).

The worm races are the highlight of the festival. Ever seen a worm race? It's about as exciting as watching paint dry on a wall. Nevertheless people pack this small town to watch the races, and to dress up their children (and dogs, cats, and potbellied pigs) as worms.

The festival is held in Vermilion in late September or early October each year. Call the Vermilion Chamber of Commerce (440-967-3467) for the date of this year's festival.

The Center of the World

WARREN

Ohio is the center of the world. If you don't believe it, just ask the Ohio Department of Transportation. They put up one of their familiar green-and-white reflecting signs proclaiming the fact. The precise "Center of the World," according to ODOT, is along a sparsely populated stretch of State Route 5, just outside of Warren.

This designation got its start in the 1840s when Randell Wilmot moved to the area from Pennsylvania. He opened up a store, stagecoach stop, bar, and lunch stand and called the complex "The Center of the World." For lonely travelers in the 1840s, the title was probably appropriate.

However, when the Cleveland and Mahoning Railroad started taking away much of his business, Wilmot closed up the Center of the World and moved east to Cortland, Ohio. There he began another business, which he called "The End of the World." That proved to be prophetic, at least for Wilmot; he died in Cortland.

Neil Armstrong Flew Here

WARREN

There is a monument to an airplane ride in Warren, Ohio. That's right, a ride.

In what is now a Kmart parking lot, there was an airport where Neil Armstrong, the first man to walk on the moon, took his very first airplane ride. The monument is a half-size model of the lunar landing module *Eagle* that Armstrong and fellow astronaut Buzz Aldrin used to land on the lunar surface.

Armstrong and his parents lived in the Warren, Ohio, area in the mid-1930s, and it was while living here that Neil Armstrong's life-long love of flight started. A visit to the Cleveland National Air Races is said to have been his first exposure to airplanes, followed by a Sunday morning flight with his father aboard a 1920s-era Ford Tri-Motor airplane, fondly known as the Tin Goose.

What is now the Kmart parking lot was the Warren Airways Airport in the 1930s.

The idea for the monument to an airplane ride was the inspiration of retired professional photographer Peter Perich of Warren. Shortly after Armstrong's moon walk, Perich commissioned an artist to do a painting depicting Armstrong and his father in front of the Ford Tri-Motor at the Warren airport. The painting was donated to the Neil Armstrong Museum in Wapakoneta, Ohio. Then Perich decided that there should be a local reminder of Warren's connection to the moon flight, and so he started on a project that took more than 30 years and the cooperation of local manufacturers, schools, and other volunteers to finally bring to completion—the building of a half-size lunar landing module.

On October 30, 2003, Neil Armstrong came back to the place where it all started, a Kmart parking lot in Warren, Ohio, and posed for a picture beside the half-size replica of his *Eagle*.

Sauerkraut Festival
WAYNESVILLE

EVENTS!

It has been reported in national publications that Ohio has more festivals than any other state. That's probably true. Pick any county, town, or village—sometime during the year they're sure to be celebrating something. Everything from flowers (the Carnation Festival in Alliance) to worms (the Woollybear Festival in Vermilion. There's the Melon Festival in Milan, the Strawberry Festival in Norwalk, the Covered Bridge Festival in Ashtabula, the Festival of the Fish in Vermilion . . .

Now, in most cases the reason is obvious: they raise a lot of the honored fruit or vegetables in that area, or are known for a great number of covered bridges. But not always.

Take Waynesville, for instance. Waynesville is known as the Antique Capital of the Midwest. It must be true—*USA Today* said so several years ago, and no other city complained or filed a counterclaim. Naturally, then, you'd expect such a town to host an antique festival. Nope. They do sauerkraut.

Why sauerkraut? They must raise a lot of cabbage around here. Nope again. Okay, a lot of German or Bavarian immigrants settled here, right? No. There's not even an obscure connection to sauerkraut here.

Back in 1970, a meeting was held among local merchants trying to stir up interest in an annual sidewalk sale. One merchant belched and said, "I had some really good sauerkraut for lunch." "I like sauerkraut, too," said another. Several others added their endorsement, and one of the merchants shouted, "Let's sponsor a sauerkraut dinner!"

The dinner grew into an annual festival, each year's event getting bigger and better until now a quarter of a million people swamp this tiny village each October to tramp past crafts booths and booths selling food—including sauerkraut candy and even ice cream. Check with the Waynesville Chamber of Commerce (513-897-8855) for festival dates.

A Victorian ATM

WELLINGTON

Most of us have used an automated teller machine. But how many of us know that the device was pioneered by an Ohio bank? In early 1970, the world's first "money machine" was installed at the City National Bank on Tremont Road in Columbus.

Now, before you start writing to tell me that *your* bank was the first to install an ATM, note this: no less an authority than the Smithsonian Institution in Washington, D.C., asked to enshrine the Columbus machine. (The Smithsonian didn't wind up with it; City National had been bought up by another bank that either couldn't find the original ATM or didn't want to donate it.)

There is another notable ATM currently on display in Ohio, though. The **LorMet Community Federal Credit Union** (216 N. Main St., Wellington; 440-647-1999) has a money machine shaped like a horse and carriage. Yep, a life-size fiberglass horse pulling a Victorian carriage (the ATM is located inside the carriage).

LorMet officials say it was the idea of their CEO, Daniel Cwalina, who wanted the modern ATM to blend in with the Victorian charm of downtown Wellington. The horse, they say, was easy to find, but a carriage that would fit over an ATM vault was another matter. They finally had to have a custom-made buggy that reaches all the way to the ground.

The display was so realistic that at first some customers thought it was just one of the many area Amish families doing a little banking. Today, most everyone has caught on.

World's Largest Cuckoo Clock

WILMOT

Alice Grossniklaus, shrewd businesswoman and amateur yodeler, wanted to draw attention to her cheese shop and restaurant. Recalling the popularity of cuckoo clocks in her native Switzerland, she decided to build one here in Wilmot. While she was at it, she decided to make it the biggest cuckoo clock ever.

According to the *Guinness Book of World Records*, she succeeded. And now, thanks to her, little Wilmot, Ohio, lays claim to being the

"Cuckoo Clock Capital of America."

It took Grossniklaus 12 years, from 1962 to 1974. She imported the nine half-life-size carved wooden figures that dance and play together in an oom-pah band on the hour and half-hour, and had a local Amish craftsman build the clock. The chiming giant is 23½ feet high, 24 feet wide, and 13½ feet deep.

Other states have claimed

larger cuckoos, but those have been buildings altered to look like clocks. This one is a true, working, stand-alone clock.

New owners now charge a fee to watch the clock strike every 30 minutes. (It's free for restaurant patrons.)

The clock is open spring through fall at **Grandma's Alpine Homestead Restaurant** (1504 U.S. Rte. 62, Wilmot; 330-359-5454).

One Big Madonna

WINDSOR

If you like your religious symbols big, I mean really big, it's hard to beat the 50-foot-tall Our Lady of Guadaloupe in Windsor.

How this statue came to rise above a rural Ohio farm is a story of faith and determination. Pat and Ed Heinz bought the 50-acre farm in 1987, but three years later when some investments went bad, the Heinzes lost the farm in bankruptcy proceedings. They moved to England so Ed could pursue work in nuclear engineering, but within just a few years they were able to move back and buy the farm again.

They decided to dedicate the farm to God and formed the **Servants of Mary Center for Peace** (6569 Ireland Rd., Windsor; 440-272-5380). They were moved to construct a statue to Our Lady of Guadaloupe alongside a small lake in the middle of the farm. It was supposed to be 30 feet high, but by the time it was completed it topped out at more than 50 feet. A lighted 1,150-foot-long illuminated rosary rings the lake in front of the statue.

The Heinzes are devout Catholics, but they say their center is open to all religions. There is a meeting hall and gift shop, and there are other shrines on the property.

The Amazing Komar
WILMOT

For 50 years he worked behind the counter in a Wilmot, Ohio, cheese shop. Most people who met him never knew his secret. Vernon Craig, a short, balding man with chin whiskers, a mild-mannered shopkeeper, has an alter ego. He travels the world and appears on television, in magazines, and newspapers . . . as "The Amazing Komar."

He holds a permanent Guinness world record for the longest fire walk in his bare feet—more than 25 feet. He also has held Guinness titles for the longest time lying on a bed of nails and the "most weight borne while lying on a bed of nails."

Vernon didn't set out to be an entertainer. Back in 1969 he was a tireless advocate for the mentally retarded. But at one point, concerned that people were listening but not hearing his message, he decided to try to get people's attention a different way—by lying down on a bed of nails.

The stunt got their attention all right. He had never tried anything like it before, and he made the bed of nails himself. When he dropped onto the nails, the tips dug into his back, and he left a trail of blood when he got up.

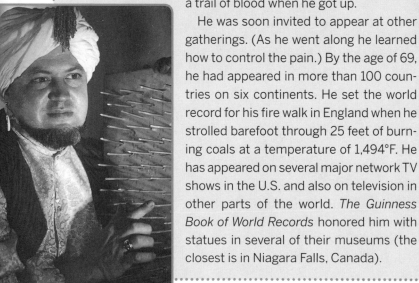

He was soon invited to appear at other gatherings. (As he went along he learned how to control the pain.) By the age of 69, he had appeared in more than 100 countries on six continents. He set the world record for his fire walk in England when he strolled barefoot through 25 feet of burning coals at a temperature of 1,494°F. He has appeared on several major network TV shows in the U.S. and also on television in other parts of the world. *The Guinness Book of World Records* honored him with statues in several of their museums (the closest is in Niagara Falls, Canada).

The President's Cemetery (That Isn't)

WOOSTER

There is a small cemetery in Wooster, Ohio, that many local folks refer to as "the president's cemetery." But not one U.S. president is buried here. So why the name?

Back in 1853 John and Elizabeth Plank of Wooster drew up a deed asking U.S. President Franklin Pierce to "hold the cemetery in trust for them and their heirs." Some people believe that the Planks, who presumably thought Wayne County, and Ohio in particular, was a fitting place for a presidential grave, were offering the cemetery to President Pierce and his family as a last resting place; others believe they wanted the president, and presumably those that came after him, to be a trustee and maintain the graves of the Plank family.

Whichever way it was, there is no record that President Pierce, who was probably preoccupied with running the country, ever considered using it or volunteered to take care of the plot for the Plank family. But you can see the original deed in the Wayne County historical records, and the cemetery is still located on Portage Road in downtown Wooster.

SOUTHEAST
OHIO

The Sign of the Cow

BARNESVILLE

Anyone who has lived on a farm knows what "the sign of the cow" is. You might unexpectedly step in it while crossing the pasture. But near Barnesville, on the south side of I-70, there is a different kind of cow sign that's a bit more interesting. It's a billboard shaped like a longhorn cow. Its owners claim it is the world's largest wooden longhorn cow.

Okay.

The cow sign is 28 feet high and 64 feet long from its tail to the tips of its longhorns. It was built by the **Dickinson Cattle Company**, which may well have the largest longhorn cattle ranch in Ohio.

They had a little problem with the tail. There was a lot of wind at the top of the hill, so they knew the slender 12-foot-long tail had to be reinforced, but with what? If they need guy wires, the cattle grazing around the sign would probably stretch the wires by using them to scratch against. Sheets of steel proved to be too heavy for the sign. Then someone had a simple idea: why not let the tail swing free, like a real cow's tail? A hinge at the top of the tail solved the problem, and now truckers driving by the huge sign on a windy night might swear the giant silhouette of a longhorn steer comes to life when its tail starts to sway in the breeze.

Riding the Range in Ohio

BARNESVILLE

The largest Texas longhorn cattle ranch east of San Francisco is right here in Ohio. The **Dickinson Cattle Company** (35500 Muskrat Rd., Barnesville; 740-758-5050) is a real, honest-to-goodness working ranch. Originally from Colorado, the Dickinsons moved their cattle ranch to Ohio in the 1990s when they purchased 5,000 acres of rolling countryside in southeast Ohio. Today a herd that often numbers over 1,500 Texas longhorn, BueLingo, and African Watusi cattle has become an inadvertent tourist attraction. The patriarch of the family, Darol Dickinson, said when they moved to Ohio they didn't realize that a working ranch would be such a novelty here. The constant interruptions by curious neighbors and passersby finally forced them to buy some old school buses and hire a tour guide and start giving tours of their ranch.

Ohio's Serengeti

CUMBERLAND

It's almost like Jurassic Park. Nearly 10,000 acres of rolling hills, valleys, and lakes are enclosed by tall, electrified security fences—to keep the beasts inside.

The Wilds (14000 International Rd., Cumberland; 740-638-5030) is a conservation, education, and science center that is home to 25 species of wildlife from Africa, Asia, and North America. Some of the animals kept here have already become extinct in the wild, and this is one of the last chances for survival of these breeds.

Located on some formerly strip-mined land once owned by utility companies, the Wilds collaborates with zoos and other wildlife conservation groups on breeding and research programs. It is open to visitors May through October. The animals range free within the enclosure; people are restricted to special buses that travel the roads.

Museum of Matchsticks

FLY

In southern Ohio, near the town of Fly, is a small museum dedicated to the life's work of a man who let a hobby get out of hand.

Jack Dempsey Johnson was a heavy-equipment operator. When medical problems caused him to retire in the 1960s, he, like so many people with time on their hands, looked for a hobby. What he found was matchsticks.

And it's what he did with the matchsticks over the next 30 years that he is remembered for. He started building things with them. First a small replica of an earthmover, then a train—complete with locomotive, two freight cars, and caboose. Then he started building replicas of buildings that he was familiar with, all Lilliputian-size, all made with matchsticks.

When he died in 1992, Johnson had constructed hundreds of tiny wooden works of art, including a replica of every building on his farm. By that time everyone in the neighborhood knew him as Matchstick Jack.

Today Matchstick Jack is gone, but his work lives on thanks to his family, who have opened the **Matchstick Jack Memorial Museum** (open by appointment only: State Rte. 800, Fly; 740-865-3035) to house his work.

The Last Washboard Manufacturer in the U.S.

LOGAN

Unless you spend a lot of time in an area where there is no running water, you may never have come in contact with a washboard. A washboard is a piece of corrugated steel or glass that you scrub clothes on. It beats scrubbing them on a rock down at the creek. Why scrub your clothes on a rock? People used to wear their clothes for several days, and believe me—they had to scrub them on some-

thing to get the smell out. Washboards also were used to make music, by scratching on the surface to keep time to folk songs.

Anyway, at one time there were dozens of washboard manufacturers in the country, but with the 1950s and the increasing popularity of automatic washers and dryers, there was a drastic drop in the sale of washboards. Most manufacturers saw the suds on the floor and went looking for a new business—all, that is, except the Columbus Washboard Company. They just ignored sliding sales and kept on making their washboards, one at a time, until, by 1999, they were the last washboard manufacturer in the country.

Despite the fact that the Amish still ordered a lot of washboards, there just wasn't a big enough market, and it looked like Columbus Washboard would finally have to call it quits too. Then an investor, George K. Richards, heard about the company and offered to buy it—lock, stock, and washboard. He put together an investment group and named Jacqui Barnett general manager.

She in turn has hired an all-female staff that does everything from cutting the boards to cutting the sheet-metal parts. (Jacqui says she has had male employees from time to time, but that they don't last long.) Oh, and they moved the company to Logan, south of Columbus, because that's where Jacqui lives, and she said she wasn't about to drive all the way to Columbus every day. They do still list the company name with a Columbus address. Today you can still find the **Columbus Washboard Company** (14 Gallagher Ave., Logan; 740-380-3828) makin' 'em one at a time. Visitors are welcome any time the factory is open. They will give free tours at the drop of a hat, just give them a call first.

Bottle-Feeding the Fish

MARIETTA

Marietta offers an exciting way to welcome spring. After watching the carp swim back up the Ohio River each April 15th, you can feed them—from baby bottles.

How do you bottle-feed a carp? One of the volunteers at the **Ohio River Museum** (601 Front St., Marietta; 800-860-0145) figured it out while working on the permanently docked sternwheeler-museum, the *W. P. Snyder Jr.* One day, while not terribly busy with museum business, he found a baby bottle someone had left onboard. Recollecting how fish made sucking noises when they ate stale bread

OHIO'S BIRTHDAY—
MARCH OR AUGUST?

The history books tell us that Ohio became a state—the first state carved out of the old Northwest Territory—on March 1, 1803. But that's not entirely correct.

The U.S. Congress never got around to formally voting on the resolution admitting Ohio to the Union until August. Of 1953.

Proponents of Ohio statehood had done a lot of lobbying in Washington, and in 1802 Congress did indeed pass the enabling bill that authorized the formation of a state government in Ohio. Citizens held a constitutional convention in Chillicothe and started sending representatives and senators to Washington. But in all the excitement Congress forgot to vote on accepting us as a new state. They didn't get around to it for 150 years.

Now some historians say it was just a formality and didn't mean anything. Nevertheless, in 1953 with a few smiles and snickers, President Dwight Eisenhower signed the resolution into law, saying he wanted Ohioans to "legally" celebrate their 150th birthday.

A Springfield, Ohio, congressman, Clarence Brown, had jokingly threatened to apply for foreign aid for Ohio if the resolution did not pass Congress this time.

But some Americans in other states didn't find it very humorous. They pointed to the number of Ohioans who had served, apparently illegitimately, as president of the United States, not to mention the countless laws and bills that had been pushed through Congress by our illegally seated representatives and senators.

The president of a Georgia college even went so far as to file a federal suit in 1984 to stop Ohioans from voting in the elections that year, claiming the 1953 action by Congress was unconstitutional. He lost the suit.

So happy birthday, Ohio, either on March 1, 1803, or August 7, 1953.

people tossed into the river, he decided to experiment. He leaned over the edge of the boat and filled the bottle with some river water. He crammed pieces of stale bread into the bottle, put the nipple back, and shook the whole mess a couple of times. Then he leaned over the edge of the boat again and offered the nipple to the fish. He suddenly found himself bottle-feeding a large three-foot-long carp.

Since then, museum staffers have picked up quite a collection of baby bottles, and they always keep a good supply of stale bread around. When tourists show up, the fish do, too. They're not dumb; when they hear footsteps they know they're going to get fed.

The carp arrive in spring, but you can try your hand at bottle-feeding them any day that the museum's open during the spring, summer, and fall.

It's Not Just a Stump—It's Public Art

MARIETTA

After a big windstorm crashed through Marietta in 1998, toppling many of the mature trees that helped win this community the designation "Tree City USA," civic leaders decided to try creating some beauty from the devastation. They hired chainsaw artist David Ferguson, from Williamstown, West Virginia, just across the Ohio River, to do something with the taller tree stumps that were still standing. He turned them into sculpture.

A month of steady sawing resulted in seven chainsaw creations on park property around the city. One of the largest shows a Native American and an early pioneer standing back to back. Another shows an eagle reclaiming his roost. Still another is called the *Critter Tree* and shows several animals peeking out from within the wrecked tree.

Ferguson said that the idea of creating public art from big stumps is spreading. He said he was also hired by a West Virginia city to turn two large tree trunks into art rather than chipping everything up and leaving just a hole in the ground. "This way the tree that has been a part of the community for many years can serve a new purpose, and it softens the loss of the shade that the tree provided," Ferguson said.

The **Marietta/Washington County Convention and Visitors Bureau** (316 Third St., Marietta; 800-288-2577) offers a map of the parks where the stump art is located.

A Really Big Muskie

MCCONNELLSVILLE

When you say "muskie," most people think of the muskellunge fish, a true fighting fish found in Ohio that grows to a length of four feet or better. Well, Ohio once was home to the largest muskie in the world—but this one wasn't a fish.

The **Big Muskie** was a piece of equipment—the second largest machine ever to "walk" the face of the earth.

The Big Muskie started life as a model 4250W Bucyrus-Erie dragline. Actually, *the* model 4250W Bucyrus-Erie—it was the only one ever built. Her 220-cubic-yard bucket weighed 230 tons—empty. She was so big that she had to be constructed on the work site—it took three years—and she started working in 1969.

Owned by the Central Ohio Coal Company, a division of American Electric Power, the giant rig once removed the earth over coal veins in strip mines, allowing bulldozers and smaller vehicles to drive right into the seams of coal and extract it. The name came about because the area being worked was mostly in Muskingum County. The Big Muskie was hard to miss even when she was working hundreds of feet from the nearest roadway. She stood nearly 20 stories high and weighed 27 million pounds. The crane operator sat in a seat five stories off the ground. The bucket that dug the earth was the size of a two-story house, and the rig was as wide as an eight-lane highway! It took 13,800 volts of electricity to run her (almost enough electricity to run a small town). And she "walked"—on hydraulic legs that moved very, very slowly. (It took her days to move just a mile.)

The Big Muskie was used until 1991, when a depression in the demand for high-sulfur Ohio coal caused her to be parked and shut down—forever, as it turned out. New laws about surface mining and new technologies had bypassed the Big Muskie. Local preservation groups tried to save the rig as a sort of tourist attraction, or a monument to the coal industry, but despite their lobbying and fundraising efforts, deadlines could not be met and demolition teams started dismantling the giant dragline in mid 1999.

Today the only thing left of the Big Muskie is the bucket. Even that alone is still quite remarkable; it's the size of an eight-lane highway and weighs over 230 tons.

After the Muskie was demolished, the bucket was hauled to a park in Morgan County owned by the electric company, on State Route 78 just east of McConnellsville, and today it sits on a hilltop as a memorial to miners who once worked this land to extract its coal.

The bucket that dug the earth was the size of a two-story house, and the rig was as wide as an eight-lane highway!

The Moonshine Capital
NEW STRAITSVILLE

There's one place in Ohio where it's legal to make moonshine.

Citizens of New Straitsville used to make really good hooch. It's said that during Prohibition, if you walked into a speakeasy in Chicago you might be asked if you wanted a local brand or a "Straitsville Special," it was that good. Today in New Straitsville, many people will boast that an uncle or a father or grandfather ran a still and supported his family during the lean years with bootleg whiskey.

Was it the water in southern Ohio? Or the whiskey-making heritage of the English, Scotch, Irish, and Welsh immigrants who settled there? One thing's for sure: the hollows, glens, abandoned coal mines, and caves around New Straitsville were perfect for the illicit operation of stills.

Prohibition ended long ago, of course, and most stills have long been dismantled. But the folks in New Straitsville don't forget. They hold a **Moonshine Festival** (New Straitsville Betterment Association, 740-394-3133) each year around Memorial Day and invite the whole world to watch moonshine being made—under a special permit, and under strict control. They can't sell it or serve it—not even sipping samples. All you can do is smell it. Then every ounce has to be destroyed under the watchful eye of state agents.

You *can* consume other things at the five-day festival—moonshine pie and moonshine cookies, for example. Some speculate that those might contain a little "sipping whiskey," just enough for flavor.

A Really, Really Big Cross

NELSONVILLE

Walter Schwartz wanted to build a memorial to his wife, Elizabeth. He wanted something special, something that everyone in the valley where they lived would see. He settled for a cross. But not just any cross. What Walter Schwartz built was a 73-foot-tall illuminated cross atop Kontner's Hill in downtown Nelsonville. When it was lighted for the first time in April 1973, it was the world's largest illuminated cross.

The Fire that Won't Go Out

NEW STRAITSVILLE

Whatever you do, don't ever tick off a coal miner. Just ask the folks in New Straitsville about the bitter, five-month-long strike between the miners and management back in 1884. The miners were unable to talk management into meeting their demands, and it made them so angry they set the mine on fire. According to historians, the angry miners put timbers in coal cars, soaked them with oil, set them ablaze, and pushed them deep into the mine on Plumber's Hill.

No one could have foreseen how big a fire they were setting.

The blaze started to burn under the ground in the thick, rich deposits of soft Ohio coal. Millions of pounds were destroyed. It is believed that the coal veins were as thick as 14 feet and ran, literally, for miles in all directions.

The fires were so intense that people could draw hot water from their wells and make coffee without a stove. Roads collapsed. Flames shot out of the ground like flaming geysers. The earth around the town started to look like outer space, with smoke and steam escaping from fissures in the earth. The fire crept under the local high school, so weakening the foundation that it had to be closed.

And the fire is still burning beneath New Straitsville after more than 115 years.

There have been several attempts to put it out. During the Great Depression, the federal Works Progress Administration spent $1 million trying to extinguish the burning coal. But there are apparently enough fractures in the rock over the coal that oxygen reaches the smoldering coal and it just keeps on burning. One local historian estimated that the coal has been burning in a 60-square-mile area around New Straitsville.

Sometimes the fire appears to have stopped, showing no evidence of burning for years. But then it breaks out in a new location. The last time was in 1991, when a hole about 15 feet across opened, and smoke and flame belched from the earth. The location, on the edge of the Wayne National Forest, took about three years to burn itself out and disappear back into the earth, where it is probably still smoldering. Some have called the New Straitsville coal fire the "longest-burning manmade fire in history."

You can see historic pictures of the fire and hear some firsthand descriptions of it from members of the **New Straitsville History Group** (200 W. Main St., New Straitsville; 740-394-2535).

ODD OHIO NAMES

Ever wonder how a town got its name? Ohio has a few that will make you stop and think. Some sound friendly and welcoming, like Charm; others, a bit tougher, like Defiance. Here are some of the oddest. They might not all still be in official use, and some may now only be crossroads, but locals still know about them.

Knockemstiff (Ross County)

Here's how a resident once explained it to me:

"Long about a hunderd years ago there was three, four taverns at the intersection, real mean places, and two of them taverns, they was each run by a lady. Well, one night a gambler from down in Portsmouth, Ohio, got into a poker game at one of the ladies' taverns and, wouldn't ya know it, he was cheatin' and the lady caught him at it. She tried to throw him outta her place, but he put up a fight and they rolled out into the middle of the road. Well, the lady across the way who run the other tavern, she saw what was happenin' and she come runnin' and jumped into the fight. All three of 'em was rollin' around on the ground, and the crowd of men was gathered round, cheerin' them on, when one of them shouted, 'Knockemstiff, ladies, knockemstiff!' And you know, everbody started to laugh, and from then on, the name of the town was Knockemstiff."

Devil Town (Wayne County)

Located just northwest of Wooster, south of the Smithville Road. It's just a local place name that was popular in the 1800s when a tannery was located there. Legend has it that on Saturday night when the workers got paid they went to the devil. Nothing left to see now.

Fly (Washington County)

This is a tiny speck on the map (no pun intended), at the end of State Route 800 where it intersects with State Route 7. It sits on the edge of the Ohio River. Local folks say it got its name because the village founders couldn't agree on a name. It was getting late when suddenly a fly landed on the chairman's desk, and he looked up and reportedly said, "Let's call it Fly." And they did.

But that's not the way Dib Harmon heard it. For thirty years, Dib has run the Fly ferryboat back and forth across the Ohio between Fly and Sisterville, West Virginia.

Dib says around the turn of the century, liquor salesmen from Marietta used to come up to Fly to take the ferry over to Sisterville. Fly didn't have a name then, but the salesmen always identified it to their customers as "that little speck, no bigger than a fly, where the ferryboat runs." He claims that people just began calling it "Fly" because of those liquor salesmen.

Take the ferry ride across the Ohio. It's a great value and a pleasant way to get to West Virginia. It costs a dollar to drive your car on board. No reservation needed. Just drive down to the edge of the Ohio and flash your headlights; Dib will bring the ferry right over to get you. He might even tell you a few stories on the way over.

Pee Pee (Pike County)

No, it's not what you think, but it is a strange name for a community. Pee Pee is located right next to Waverly, Ohio, in the southern part of the state. There isn't much there; just a motor-

cycle shop and a service station, which sells bumper stickers that proclaim "I got gas in Pee Pee, Ohio."

And of course, there is the problem of what to call the local residents. "Pee Peeans?"

I noticed a certain reluctance on the part of some residents to acknowledge the name. Their township garage has a very small sign, and none of the community-owned vehicles have any kind of township name painted on the sides. In fact, the only other place I could find the name was on a sign, put up by the state, pointing out Pee Pee Creek. It boggles my mind to think about what the sight of all that running water does to people searching for the community of Pee Pee.

Like I said, it's not what you think. Actually, the name was derived from the town's founder, Major Paul Paine, who carved his initials on a tree along the creek. In time, "P. P." became "Pee Pee."

The folks at the gas station think the name is great and love to capitalize on it, but many of the other folks in the community don't think it's very funny.

The Funniest Intersection in America

WEST CHESTER

The funniest intersection in America is located in Ohio, according to the State Farm Insurance company. The insurance giant researches the most dangerous intersections in America, and they have listed the funniest name combinations they found. Their number one? The intersection of Grinn and Barrett in West Chester.

The Y Bridge

ZANESVILLE

It's been called the bridge to nowhere. Some people say it just doesn't make much sense, but the **Y Bridge** in Zanesville has been an Ohio curiosity for nearly two hundred years. It truly is a bridge in the shape of a "Y" that crosses both the Licking and Muskingum rivers. The first version of the bridge was built back in 1814; the present steel and concrete structure is the fifth Y-shaped bridge to be built in this location.

Why the "bridge to nowhere"? Well, this may be the only bridge in the world that you can cross and still end up back on the same side of the river where you started—it's clear if you look at an aerial shot of the bridge.

The Y Bridge is on Route 40 in downtown Zanesville, and you can get a good look at it from on high in nearby Putnam Hill Park.

SOUTHWEST
OHIO

The Cradle of Dentistry

BAINBRIDGE

The "Cradle of Dentistry" is, according to the Ohio Dental Association, in Bainbridge. There, in 1827, Dr. John Harris opened the first dental school in the U.S. Now it's home to the **John Harris Dental Museum** (open Saturday and Sunday afternoons or by appointment, 208 W. Main St., Bainbridge; 740-634-2228). Exhibits include items used by dentists two hundred years ago that look appropriate for a torture chamber in some dungeon. (Harris's brother, Chapin, also a dentist, was one of the founders of the Baltimore College of Dental Surgery in 1840.)

World's Largest Horseshoe Crab

BLANCHESTER

Motorists driving along Ohio Route 28 in Blanchester sometimes don't believe their eyes. There, in a parking lot next to the **Freedom Worship Baptist Church**, stands a giant horseshoe crab (664 W. Main St./State Rte. 28, Blanchester; 513-256-5437). The coral-colored monster crab is 68 feet long, 28 feet wide, and 13 feet tall. The interior of the crab can seat up to 65 people—which makes Jonah's whale sound like a sardine.

Horseshoe crabs are usually found in the Gulf of Mexico, the Delaware Bay, or along the Atlantic seaboard. So what the heck is the world's largest horseshoe crab doing in Ohio—a long way from any salt water?

The rather complex story began when the maritime museum on the Inner Harbor in Baltimore, Maryland, contracted with a firm that designed some of Disney World's attractions to build a huge replica of horseshoe crab. Shortly after the crab was delivered, though, the museum had some financial difficulties. The crab was cut into nine large pieces and put into storage. There it remained for a while until it was purchased by the Creation Museum in Petersburg, Kentucky. The giant crab was due to be reassembled next to the new museum, but then they needed to expand the parking lot and it was decided that the crab was taking up too much space. That's when Pastor Jim Rankin of the Freedom Worship Baptist Church in Blanchester, Ohio, got involved.

Rankin had been invited to speak to the staff of the Creation Museum, and following his talk museum officials took him to the parking lot and offered to donate the big crab to his church. He accepted, and just days later five tractor-trailer rigs loaded with huge fiberglass and foam crab parts arrived in Blanchester. With the help of a crane, the world's largest horseshoe crab was finally back together again at its new home in a garden outside the Blanchester church.

Why, you might ask, would either a creation museum or a church in Ohio want an enormous replica of a crab? That's easy: the evolution debate. According to Pastor Rankin, the horseshoe crab has not evolved. It looks the same today as it did at the beginning of time, and that helps bolster the argument against the theory of evolution. It is now the centerpiece of a garden devoted to Creation and biblical scripture. Also, the crab can host weddings.

Flying Saucer Home
CARLISLE

In Carlisle, south of Columbus, passersby at the corner of Central and Chamberlain do a double-take: there sit two flying saucers connected by a silver tube. It's actually a private home.

World's Largest Swimming Pool
CINCINNATI

This swimming pool is so big that the lifeguards have to patrol it from small boats. **Sunlite Pool at Coney Island Park** (6201 Kellogg Ave., Cincinnati; 513-232-8230) near Cincinnati is reported to be the largest recirculating pool in the world—400 feet long and 200 feet wide, holding 3 million gallons of water and accommodating 10,000 swimmers at one time. It also features a 500-foot-long water slide. The depth ranges from six inches to 10 feet.

When the owner decided to build Kings Island Amusement Park north of downtown Cincinnati, many of the Coney Island rides were moved there, and it looked like the end of the road for this riverside attraction. But Cincinnatians wouldn't let it die. They had too many memories of wonderful summers there, and over the years the pool and the associated park have made a comeback. Today, the biggest recirculating pool on earth is again part of a full-fledged amusement park, run by new owners.

Tiny Little Cincinnati

CINCINNATI

They've shrunk downtown Cincinnati to an area about the size of a football field at the **Cincinnati History Museum** (Cincinnati Museum Center, 1301 Western Ave., Cincinnati; 800-733-2077).

It's reproduced at one sixty-fourth of its size. The city's skyscraper, the Carew Tower building, is replicated at a height of about 7 feet.

Miniature cars and trolleys move on the streets, darkness falls, and the lights go on in the city. There is even a vacant lot with a small boy flying a kite and a house that appears to catch fire. You'll feel like Gulliver having his first view of Lilliput when you get your first look at "Cincinnati in Motion." (History moves here also: at the

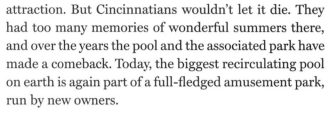

Ohio River side of the city the time is 1940, but as you go away from the river, the years drop away until you end in the suburbs in the year 1900.)

Porker Paradise

EVENTS!

EATON

Cincinnati once shipped so many pigs through its river port that it was known the world over as "Porkopolis." But today that title might be better suited to Preble County, home of the **Preble County Pork Festival** (Preble County Fairgrounds, 722 S. Franklin St., Eaton; 937-456-7273), held every year on the third full weekend in September.

Pork farmers here take this festival seriously. There can be as many as 2,500 pork chops on the grill at one time. The 4-H Club sells sugar waffles shaped like pigs. They even have a "Porkville" country store where you can buy fresh pork loin. Sunday after church services they hold several heats of the popular pig races.

The highlight of the festival comes when they put on a sausage-making demonstration. The old-fashioned way. Visitors can actually watch them slaughter a hog, then cut it up and grind up portions to make fresh sausage. (Do the losers of those pig races get chosen to demonstrate the sausage making?)

Little girls are encouraged to wear pigtails, and there is a contest for the best pigtail. The festival's motto is: "The next time you eat a pork chop or see a pig, think of Preble County Pork Festival."

Buried in a Potato Chip Can

CINCINNATI, OHIO

Frederic J. Baur had much to be proud of in his life: he was an acclaimed organic chemist and had a doctorate in that field. He worked for many years in research and development at Procter and Gamble, the corporate colossus of Cincinnati. But Baur, who passed away in 2008 at age 89, was proudest of creating a package for potato chips. He was the man who invented the Pringles potato chip can. In fact, he was so proud of the little round can that holds stacked, processed potato chips that he asked to be cremated when he died and have his remains buried in a Pringles can. His family decided he was serious about the matter, so upon his death some of his ashes were deposited in a bright-red original Pringles potato chip can and buried (along with more of his remains in a formal urn) at **Arlington Memorial Gardens** (2145 Compton Rd., Cincinnati; 513-521-7003).

All the Presidents' Planes

FAIRBORN

Dayton has an exhibit that must make other aerospace museums green with envy.

They have four of the five retired primary aircraft dedicated to supporting the president, plus five additional aircraft used by the presidents since World War II.

Dayton is the home of Wright-Patterson Air Force Base, which has the largest and oldest military aviation museum in the world: the **U.S. Air Force Museum** (Wright-Patterson Air Force Base, 1100 Spaatz Ave., Fairborn; 937-255-3286). All airplanes used by the president of the United States are air force planes, so it naturally follows that when they retire, they head for Ohio and the Air Force Museum.

By the time the air force started sending presidential planes to Dayton, the museum there was already crammed with other historic

planes. (Its collection now includes a B-52 bomber, a Stealth Fighter, and hundreds of others.) There just wasn't room in the hangar for presidential aircraft, so the planes have been relegated to an old World War II-era hangar that the museum uses for storage.

You can make a reservation to catch the shuttle bus to visit the Presidential Hangar. (Be prepared: the hangars are not air-conditioned and are crowded with many other planes; during the height of the summer tourist season, it can get mighty hot inside.)

Top billing goes to SAM 26000. Does that ring a bell? That big blue-and-silver 707 was used as Air Force One by eight presidents— from John F. Kennedy to Bill Clinton. It holds the distinction of being the aircraft on which Lyndon Johnson was inaugurated as president in 1963 while the plane was on the ground at Love Field in Dallas, shortly after President Kennedy was assassinated.

In addition to Kennedy's Air Force One, you can also see *Columbine III*, the Super Constellation that Dwight Eisenhower used; Harry S. Truman's *Independence*; and the very first presidential airplane, a World War II VC-54C used by Franklin Roosevelt—known as *The Sacred Cow*. (An elevator was installed in the aircraft to get FDR aboard in his wheelchair.)

Admission to the Air Force Museum is free, as is admission to see the presidential aircraft, but you must have a reservation and must use their shuttle bus.

The King of Halloween

FAIRBORN

Time warp! Time warp! That's what your mind will be telling you as you walk into this dime store in Fairborn. The candy case, with its candy corn, root-beer barrels, and bridge mix, is just inside the front door. The floors are wooden and show the passage of time. You can find the traditional things you always found at the dime store: pins and thread, brooms and mops, cards and lace. There's even a pet department where you can buy a small bird. Like all dime stores it's cluttered, with merchandise piled to the ceiling—in some cases its hanging from the ceiling.

Foy's Variety Store (18 E. Main St., Fairborn; 937-878-0671) is a Fairborn institution. It was founded in 1929 by Mike Foy, the present owner's grandfather, and remained pretty much unchanged until the last part of the 20th century, when Mike Foy took over.

Mike, you see, *loves* Halloween, and while the dime store had always carried a small selection of Halloween masks and costumes, Mike decided to enlarge the Halloween department. And, boy, did he ever!

Mike Foy has now taken over almost two city blocks in downtown Fairborn, converting former stores into Halloween specialty shops.

One store sells nothing but children's costumes. Another rents and sells costumes for adults. A former bar has been turned into a store for commercial "haunted house" paraphernalia, things like rubber dummies in electric chairs and jail cells with monsters inside fighting to get out. You can buy plastic life-size skeletons here. A former pool hall has been reborn as a diner right out of the 1950s, a neat place to grab a snack while shopping for Halloween goodies.

Last I heard, Mike was negotiating with local realtors for an abandoned granary elevator up the street. "Wouldn't that make a great haunted house?" he asked.

You can't miss Mike's stores when you drive into downtown Fairborn. Just look for the place with the inflatable gorilla on top, next to the one where the skeleton is hanging from the roof. There are also several vintage hearses parked on the street.

The Wacky Grocer

FAIRFIELD

How unusual can a grocery store be? How unusual do you want it? In Fairfield, Jim Bonaminio, known to his customers as "Jungle" Jim, takes great pains to make sure you don't mistake his store— **Jungle Jim's International Market** (5440 Dixie Hwy., Fairfield; 513-674-6000)—for any ordinary one.

For openers, it's big—more than four acres under one roof—but that's not what sets it apart. There's the personality of its owner, Jungle Jim. You can often find him gliding up and down the aisles on roller skates, wearing one of his many costumes. One visit found him dressed as a cowboy on roller skates, with chaps, a western shirt, a hat, and a gun belt. But in the holster, instead of a six-shooter he had a foot-long leek, which he used as a pointer.

And there's entertainment. In the seafood department is a 40-foot cabin cruiser that has seen better days, painted up to be the *S.S. Minnow* and containing an animated band of cartoon characters that break into song every few minutes. There is a singing animatronic Elvis lion, and a pair of electronic crows that burst into "Rockin' Robin" every five minutes or so.

Against a back wall of the store, past several rows of specialty foods from around the world, there's a small movie theater that continuously plays—what else?—*The Jungle Jim Story: Evolution of the Jungle.*

The shelves hold products you won't find in many stores, from water canned from a spring at the base of Mt. Fuji to a box of fresh cactus leaves. Jim has become famous for the sheer number of things he carries—more than 110,000 different food items from more than 72 countries. He was among the first grocers to introduce a mushroom bar (like a salad bar, but just for mushrooms).

Gummy Walls

GREENVILLE

You've been working that big wad of Doublemint in your jaw all morning, and the flavor is finally just about gone. It's lunchtime, and you're pulling up at the **Maid-Rite Sandwich Shop** (125 N. Broadway St., Greenville; 937-548-9340). What to do with the gum? As you head toward the drive-up window, just reach out your window and smack it against the brick building.

Sounds gross, but that's what people have been doing for years. So much so that the walls have taken on the look of a gum sculpture. No one is quite sure just how the custom started, but as they sang in *Fiddler on the Roof*, it's "tradition." Not only don't they scrape it off, they seem to encourage it.

Must help you get your appetite prepared for their featured menu item: "Loose Meat Sandwiches." I'm not exactly sure what "loose meat" means, but an employee said they serve as many as 400 per hour.

Special on "ABC" gum at the Maid-Rite! (Get your juices flowing for the loose meat sandwich.)

Pyramid Hill Sculpture Park

HAMILTON

Harry T. Wilks, a retired attorney from Hamilton, likes his art BIG.

Wilks bought 45 acres of wooded land for a home and built a beautiful underground home in the side of a hill. Then he bought more land. And then he got the idea to build a park for sculptures. Not just any sculptures—really *big* sculptures. Thus **Pyramid Hill Sculpture Park** (State Rte. 128, Hamilton; 513-868-8336) was born. He kept on buying adjoining land, adding up to 265 acres of hilly property.

Today at this non-profit arts and cultural center, there are more than three dozen enormous works of art placed on hills and in valleys. The largest is *Abracadabra*, by Alexander Liberman. The vast, twisted red metal sculpture is two-and-a-half stories tall and nearly four stories wide. Pilots landing at nearby Cincinnati Regional Airport have said they can easily see it from the air.

A Man's Castle Is His Home
LOVELAND

In 1973, Harry Andrews, who never married and had no family, decided to start a band of knights. Conveniently, he already had his own castle.

The dream actually started in Loveland right after the first world war. Andrews returned from Europe enchanted by the wondrous sights he had seen—especially the castles in England and France. He daydreamed about them until 1927, when he decided to make his fantasy come true.

Andrews taught Sunday school to a group of teenagers. He would occasionally take them to a favorite swimming hole along the Little Miami River, where they would camp out, fish and swim. Andrews eventually bought the property and challenged the youngsters to help him build what he originally called "a stone tent."

The kids helped carry buckets of stones and sand from the river to the construction site. Two small stone rooms were completed by 1929, just as the Great Depression swept the country. As hard times moved across Ohio, many of the youngsters went off to work in the Civilian Conservation Corps; work on the building slowed. And as some families broke up due to lack of work and money, Andrews found himself caring for some of the youngsters who used to be in his Sunday school class. He would regale them with stories of the great castles he had seen during his wartime service. As the Depression eased, Andrews had a new vision: his "stone tents" would become the base of his very own castle.

Bucket by bucket of stones and sand, the castle grew over the next 30 years. He gave it a name, **Chateau La Roche** (12025 Shore Dr., Loveland; 513-683-4686)—"house of stone." Today it's a three-story castle surrounded by four-story-high battle towers. And most of the work was done by one man: Harry Andrews. In the 1950s,

Andrews gave up his job and devoted the rest of his life to working on the castle. Eventually he discovered that without meaning to, he had created a tourist attraction. Frequently while he was working alone on the building, carloads of the curious would stop by and ask questions or want to take pictures. By the late 1970s, upward of 50,000 people per year were stopping by. Something had to be done.

That's when Andrews incorporated the Knights of the Golden Trail and directed that upon his death the knights would take over ownership of the castle and grounds.

Monument to a Pig

MIDDLETOWN

Just outside of Middletown is a tribute to a pig. Not just *a* pig, actually, but a whole race of pigs. Namely, the Poland China hog.

It was on a farm here that the very first Poland China hog in the nation was bred and born. The breed was so successful that today

Poland China hogs are popular all over the world. A six-foot-tall stone monument to the hog was erected near the original farm. (A shopping mall was erected *on* the farm, but you can still see the memorial across from the entrance to Towne Mall on Route 25 if you look carefully.)

For more information about the hog statue, try the **Middletown Historical Society** (56 S. Main St., Middletown; 513-424-5539).

Jesus Rising

MONROE

A sixty-two-foot-tall fiberglass statue of Jesus appears to rise out of a reflecting pond alongside I-75 in Warren County. It is believed to be the largest sculpture of Christ in North America.

The sculpture actually stands in front of the **Solid Rock Church of Monroe** (904 N. Union Rd., Monroe, Ohio). It was created by artist James Lynch, who has done other huge sculptures in places like Disney World and Las Vegas. Lynch made an original sculpture out of foam plastic in his Jacksonville, Florida studio. From that a mold was made for creating the final fiberglass sculpture, which was then shipped to Monroe and assembled on the spot in 2004.

The Missing Body

NORTH BEND

Ohio has a lot of presidential stories. After all, the state competes with Virginia for the title "Mother of Presidents." But there is one presidential story that is rarely told, involving a man who was the son of one U.S. president and the father of another.

John Scott Harrison was the son of the first U.S. president from Ohio, William Henry Harrison (who holds the record for the shortest term of office: he died after being in office only 30 days), and the father of Benjamin Harrison.

John Scott died at the age of 74 in 1878. It was a time when doctors were not allowed to use human remains to practice on, so the grim business of grave robbing was relied on to supply medical schools. Grave robbers closely watched the obituaries in the paper, then snuck into a cemetery after a funeral to dig up the fresh body.

The Harrison family, aware of this danger, took precautions when they buried John Scott in the North Bend cemetery. His grave contained a cemented brick vault, and after his casket was lowered into it, it was covered with logs and stones to make removal difficult.

A week after Harrison was buried, his family heard that the body of a neighbor, Augustus Devin, was missing from the same cemetery. Suspecting that nearby medical schools were responsible, the Harrison family led a posse into Cincinnati. At the Medical College of Ohio, they discovered a hidden trap door and, behind it, a nude body hanging upside down by a rope.

When they pulled the sheet from the face of the cadaver, the Harrisons found themselves staring not at their neighbor but at their own father, John Scott Harrison. They later found the body of Augustus Devin in a pickle barrel filled with brine.

The discovery and the resulting publicity across the country led to a change in laws allowing medical schools to use donated and unclaimed bodies for scientific purposes. It finally brought an end to grave robbing.

As for John Scott Harrison, his family reinterred him in the vault with his father, William Henry Harrison, behind barred doors and with no marker on whichever crypt held his body. You can still see the tomb of both Harrisons in North Bend, overlooking the Ohio River.

For information contact the **Ohio Historical Society** (1982 Velma Ave., Columbus; 614-297-2300).

The Serpent Mound

PEEBLES

A mysterious 1,330-foot-long serpent twists and turns through gentle Ohio countryside in Adams County. **Serpent Mound** (3850 State Rte. 73, Peebles; 800-752-2757) is known all over the world. Historians believe it was built by the Adena Indians about 2,000 years ago, but since there is no written history of that culture, no one is sure. The mound gets its name from its shape; from above it looks like an uncoiling serpent with an egg in its mouth. Why it was built has always puzzled investigators. Was it for religious rites, or as sort of an early calendar? While no evidence of burials has been found in the Serpent Mound, nearby conical mounds did contain bodies of the Adena people dating back to around 800 B.C.

Today you can best see the Serpent Mound from an observation tower on the grounds.

HOME OF UNDERWEAR GREATNESS

PIQUA

A historical marker just outside Piqua commemorates Don Gentile, World War II Army Air Force fighter ace, as the local hero. But the rest of the world probably knows Piqua best as the home of a <u>super</u>hero: Captain Underpants.

Dav Pilkey, author of the *Captain Underpants* children's book series (most popular with the fourth-grade crowd), wrote "I chose Piqua because they have an Underwear Festival there every year. It seemed like the perfect place!"

Sadly, they *used* to have an Underwear Festival. But no more. The festival hasn't been held since 1997 because of declining attendance, reported the Piqua Chamber of Commerce.

Why did Piqua celebrate underwear in the first place? It's the birthplace of the union suit, that red, one-piece long john with the flap in the seat—invented locally by the Atlas Underwear Company (or possibly one of eight other competing underwear companies operating in Piqua during the early part of the twentieth century—they all took credit for it at one time or another).

General Grant's Wandering Home

POINT PLEASANT

Ohio has a wealth of presidential history. Maybe that's why we're a bit casual with some of our historic sites. Take Ulysses S. Grant's birthplace, a tiny cottage on the Ohio River at Point Pleasant in Clermont County.

To be fair, Grant was born here and lived in the building for less than a year before the family moved on to a bigger home in nearby Georgetown. But it was still his birthplace, and those sorts of things are usually kept track of, at least for presidents.

Not much was ever made of the place until after Grant had helped win the Civil War and served as president of the United States. Then, in the late 1800s, enterprising souls decided to make a buck on the birthplace. They put it on a large barge and floated it up and down the Ohio, Missouri, and Mississippi rivers, charging admission to see the actual house where Grant was born.

Then, if that wasn't indignity enough, in the 1920s the little building was torn down, loaded on flatcars, and taken to Columbus, where it was reconstructed as an exhibit at the Ohio State Fair. The building got pretty shabby from lack of attention during the Great Depression until in 1936 it was rescued, taken down again, returned to Point Pleasant, and reconstructed on its original foundation.

Today **President Grant's birthplace** (U.S. Rte. 52, Point Pleasant; 513-553-4911) is on the National Register of Historic Places, and that should keep it in one place for a while.

Leonard Slye from Duck Run

PORTSMOUTH

Ohio can claim to be the birthplace of at least two kings: "King of Hollywood" Clark Gable (see "A King Was Born Here," Cadiz) and "King of the Cowboys" Roy Rogers.

Rogers was crowned king through a bit of press-agent gimmickry during World War II, when rival singing cowboy Gene Autry was serving in the U.S. Air Force and unable to make movies. Rogers was America's most popular cowboy at the box office for 12 straight years. He made more than 80 movies. He recorded songs and made television appearances—there were books and comic books, furniture, lunch buckets, toys, you-name-it, stamped with his name and likeness.

Heady stuff for a guy who started out as Leonard Frank Slye from Cincinnati, Ohio. He spent his childhood in a community called Duck Run, in Scioto County near Portsmouth. It was from here that his family packed up and decided to move to California during the Great Depression.

Roy's Cincinnati birthplace was torn down years ago to make way for Cynergy Field, but you can still see the home he grew up in near Portsmouth (although it is a private residence and there are no tours). In downtown Portsmouth there is the Roy Rogers Esplanade, with a concrete slab that contains Rogers's footprints and handprints from a public appearance he once made in town.

The Shoelace Capital

PORTSMOUTH

If you wear shoelaces, chances are they were made in Ohio. Portsmouth is home to the world's largest manufacturer of shoelaces.

Now you might think a shoelace factory isn't a big deal, but **Mitchellace, Inc.** (830 Murray St., Portsmouth; 740-354-2813) occupies a 360,000-square-foot factory. The plant, several stories high and covering a city block, produces more than four million pairs of shoelaces every week.

Ah, pairs. Did you know that you can't buy just one shoestring? That marketing gimmick was started many years ago by Mitchellace (which has been around since 1902). They pack two laces to a package so you always have to buy an extra one.

Aunt Jemima Was Once a Buckeye

RIPLEY

Aunt Jemima wasn't a real person, just an advertising gimmick to sell self-rising pancake flour. But real people were hired to portray her. The first was Nancy Green, hired in 1893 at the Columbian Exposition in Chicago to wear a bandanna on her head and make and promote the pancakes. After she died in an auto accident in 1923, Quaker Oats started hiring other women to promote the pancake mix. One of these was Rosa "Rosie" Riles of Ripley. Riles was tapped to portray Aunt Jemima in ads, and she also made personal appearances all through Ohio, Indiana, Illinois, and Kentucky. She died in 1969 and is buried in the **Red Oak Presbyterian Church** cemetery, near Ripley. The church has a small exhibit on Riles's career as Aunt Jemima.

(Cough!) The Tobacco Museum (Cough!)

RIPLEY

Yes—hack! *cough!*—there is—*cough!*—really a tobacco museum in Ohio.

Suitably enough, it's called **The Tobacco Museum** (703 S. Second St., Ripley; 937-392-9410). Located in southeast Ohio, where tobacco was once a major farm crop, it celebrates tobacco farming and the

Smoke, Smoke, Smoke
RIPLEY

Got someone in the family who just can't live without lighting up? Someone who refuses to go to a restaurant that doesn't allow smoking? Here's the place for them.

The **Ohio Tobacco Festival** (937-373-3651) is held in Ripley, usually in late August.

There's a lot of tobacco grown in southern Ohio, and this is one place where smoking is definitely allowed.

The festival includes tobacco worm races, a tobacco stripping and plugging contest, a garden-tractor obstacle race, and—fun for the whole family—a tobacco spitting contest.

Can't get enough smoke at the festival? Try the Ohio Tobacco Festival Museum (703 S. Second St., Ripley; 937-392-9410).

tobacco variety that was once native to Ohio: white burley. Visitors can learn that even one of our presidents, Thomas Jefferson, was once a tobacco farmer. One of the rooms displays the early equipment used to produce tobacco. There are also some antique tools on display as well as a nicely restored Federal period home where the museum is housed.

The Man Who Built a Roller Coaster

ROSS

You have to admire Ralph Stricker. He's one of those single-minded people who make their minds up to do something and won't let anything or anyone stop them. Not even his wife.

Ralph wanted to build a roller coaster in his cornfield.

He doesn't particularly like to *ride* roller coasters, mind you, but he had always been fascinated by the way the big wooden coasters were put together, almost like a giant jigsaw puzzle.

Ralph worked most of his adult life at Procter & Gamble as a stationary engineer. He was also a pretty fair self-taught carpenter.

As he neared retirement, he would go to amusement parks like Kings Island, but instead of riding the roller coasters, he would just stand and study them from many different angles. He eventually

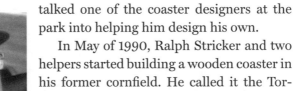

talked one of the coaster designers at the park into helping him design his own.

In May of 1990, Ralph Stricker and two helpers started building a wooden coaster in his former cornfield. He called it the Tornado. The work went on summer and winter. Ralph and his helpers hauled long timbers to their barn so they could build "bents," the legs of wooden roller coasters. From an old amusement park in Florida he obtained the chains and gears to work the ride. He finally

bought new cars from the Philadelphia Toboggan Company, the firm that specializes in roller-coaster cars.

In June of 1993, Ralph finally stood atop his highest hill. The coaster, 55 feet tall and 2,080 long, was done.

To a real coaster fan, used to two- and three-hundred-foot drops, that might seem pretty tame. But Ralph Stricker built this one himself.

I had a chance to ride Ralph's "Tornado" once. While it may not compete with Kings Island's The Beast or Cedar Point's Magnum, it's a good, solid wooden coaster that gives a decent ride and even a little airtime (little hills that launch you out of your seat for a second or two). I was having a great time, but when I looked over my shoulder at Ralph, who was riding behind me, he had no expression on his face at all. I asked him later if he was enjoying himself, and he replied, "I just build 'em, I don't ride 'em."

In fact, Ralph enjoyed building the "Tornado" so much that the next year he started building a second roller coaster, a scaled-down version called the "Teddy Bear."

Ralph Stricker decided to build it whether they come or not, for the sheer pleasure of creating his very own roller coaster.

Stricker's Grove (11490 Hamilton-Cleves Rd. / Ohio Rte. 128, Ross; 513-738-3366), which has Ralph's roller coaster and a dozen or so other mechanical rides, is open for corporate rentals during the summer and open to the public on only two days, the Fourth of July and the second Sunday in August.

Creating the World with a Hammer

SPRINGFIELD

Ben Hartman of Springfield just wanted to build a small fishpond in his backyard. It was the Great Depression, and he was out of work and wanted to keep busy. But that small cement-and-stone fishpond grew into an obsession that kept him building the rest of his life.

After the fishpond, he decided to build a miniature version of the "Little Church Around the Corner," the famous New York City landmark. Then he decided to build a small replica of a country schoolhouse. After that, said his widow, Mary Hartman, he just "always seemed to be working on something, he had all these ideas."

Christ on Calvary joined the Barbara Fritchie home (where she defied Stonewall Jackson). Independence Hall in Philadelphia was built near Flanders Field from the First World War.

Hartman got the stones to build his world from a nearby housing development where fields were being cleared of rocks. He'd bring them back to his workshop and break them into small pieces with a hammer. In seven years he wore out three hammers.

He built a four-foot-high

WHAT TIME IS IT?

UNION CITY

What time is it? That's a simple question, unless you're in Union City. Then it depends on which side of the street you live on.

You see, Union City, Ohio, and Union City, Indiana, share a lot of things, including the Ohio-Indiana border. It looks like one small town, but it acts like two. They have two city halls, two police and fire departments, and even two school systems.

But what really sets them apart is Daylight Savings Time. Ohio uses it, but Indiana doesn't, remaining on Eastern Standard Time. So summertime in Union City can get a bit confusing, even for longtime residents.

For example, anyone advertising a local event must specify the time in both Ohio and Indiana times if they hope to attract a crowd on time. Taverns on the Ohio side of the line have to close an hour earlier than their counterparts just a block away. Heck, some people who walk to their jobs leave home nearly an hour after they get to work. Huh?

stone cup and saucer. He created a replica in stone of the birthplace of Abraham Lincoln. There was Custer's Last Stand, and Noah's Ark.

When curious neighbors and passersby who had heard of the project would stop over, Hartman would stop working and show them around. If someone pressed a coin into his hand when they left, he would save it until he had enough to buy another bag of cement and build some more. He even built a castle eight feet high and six feet wide, complete with moat and drawbridge. It took 14,000 stones to do that.

In all, Ben Hartman crushed up a quarter of a million stones, one at a time, to build his hundreds and hundreds of statues, figures, and buildings.

Ben Hartman died a long time ago, in 1944, and time has eroded some of his little world. But Mary still plants flowers around her yard and welcomes strangers who want to see what one man and three hammers could accomplish.

The **Hartman Rock Garden** is on the corner of McKaw and Russell streets in Springfield. According to the Springfield Vistors' Bureau (937-325-7621), visitors are welcome. Hours are whenever someone is at home.

Trapshooters Hall of Fame

VANDALIA

It probably surprises no one that legendary Ohio sharpshooter Annie Oakley was one of the first persons inducted into the **Trapshooter's Hall of Fame** (601 W. National Rd., Vandalia; 937-898-4638) in Vandalia. But what the heck is John Philip Sousa doing here? It turns out that the famed military band leader also loved trapshooting—and was darn good at it, too. Trapshooting—using shotguns to shoot clay disks fired into the air at blazing speeds—requires quick reflexes and a good eye. In the Trapshooter's Hall of Fame and Museum, beside pictures and biographies of the inductees, you'll find historic weapons and early trapshooting gear as well as collections of shotgun shells and boxes.

Ohio's "Most Perfect Tree"

WAVERLY

Waverly claims to be the home of Ohio's "most perfect tree." The 200-year-old hard maple is the lead item in the local tourist bureau's brochure.

No one is sure just who first noticed that the tree was perfect.

"Old-timers here swear they have always known," wrote Linda Basye, who runs the **Pike County Convention and Visitors Bureau** (12455 State Rte. 104, Waverly; 740-947-9650). "But no paperwork has turned up, aside from some early newspaper clippings that also refer to it as '**Ohio's Perfect Tree**.'"

She suspects that the designation dates back to the late 1800s, when Pike County had some political influence in the state.

The tree is located on State Route 355, just 3½ miles south of the intersection with State Route 32. It's on private property, but the Ohio Department of Transportation has thoughtfully carved out a three-car parking area from which the tree can easily be seen.

A Funeral Home Museum

WEST UNION

The **William Lafferty Memorial Funeral and Carriage Collection** (205 Cherry St., West Union; 937-544-2121) contains not only old horse-drawn hearses from the nineteenth century but also a collection of the various tools that undertakers have used over the last hundred years or so. Things like burial clothing, shrouds, even old wooden caskets and embalming kits.

The collection was started years ago by William Lafferty, who operated a funeral home in West Union, Ohio. He began with a horse-drawn hearse he had once used in the family business. Then he started going to carriage auctions and buying more ornate funeral buggies. For years the collection was scattered in several garages and outbuildings, until finally, after Lafferty's death, his wife, Grace, together with his son John Lafferty and John's wife, Elaine, decided to construct a building to display all of the late William Lafferty's collection. The result is a collection of nine carriages and hundreds of other items, such as early funeral-home ledgers and even handwritten instructions from some of his customers for the disposition of their remains.

The First Banana Split

WILMINGTON

Turf wars have erupted over some pretty silly things through the years. Like, who has the biggest ball of string? Or, where was the first cheeseburger cooked? But when they start talking about ice cream, one thing's for sure: Ohio is the birthplace of the banana split.

The good folks in Wilmington have been making that claim since the beginning of the last century. It was old "Doc" Hazard at Hazard's Drug Store who one day decided to add a banana to a rather large ice-cream sundae. He wanted to make it look even bigger, so he cut the banana lengthwise into two pieces and called it a "banana split."

Disregard the folks in Latrobe, Pennsylvania, who are "Johnny-come-latelys" to the banana split wars. They claim the dessert was invented in a drug store in their town in 1905, but by the time they announced this, Wilmington had already put in its claim for the honor, citing 1907 as the date the delicacy was first created.

To cement their claim, Wilmington holds a Banana Split Festival each year on the second weekend in June, and thousands of people flock to the town to sample a banana split the way it was made back in 1907. For information, call the Clinton County Convention and Visitors' Bureau (877-428-4748). **Gibson's Goodies** (718 Ohio Ave., Wilmington; 937-383-2373) claims to have the original banana split recipe.

A slice of history: The original banana split recipe, according to Gibson Goodies in Wilmington.

ACKNOWLEDGMENTS

There aren't enough words to say thank you to all the folks who helped make this book possible. I do want to pay tribute here to some of the folks who went above and beyond and over and above and all those good things to help me.

Tim Wrenn of Sandusky dragged me around the Lake Erie islands in his brand-new boat so I could get a close-up picture of the *Benson Ford*, the incredible boat home on the shores of South Bass Island. My good friend Carl Feather of Ashtabula, a gifted author and journalist, offered me many ideas and suggestions for the book. There was also David Giffels, the popular and talented columnist with the *Akron Beacon Journal*, who was kind enough to give me space in his columns several times and urge his readers to send me their weirdest and most curious stories. (One of his readers suggested his whole family would qualify as weird!) Thanks to them we uncovered the story of Queen Victoria's underpants in the Kent State University Museum, and David reminded me of the uniqueness of the historic Akron dirigible airdock, along with many other ideas.

Thanks to Richard Rolenz of Akron for the tip on the hearing aid museum at Kent State University, and Bob Hines in Columbus for suggesting the story of Chic-Chic, the chicken who bought his own lunch.

I'm grateful to historian Roger Bridges, curator Jay Snider, and Thomas Culbertson of the Hayes Presidential Center in Fremont for answering countless questions and doing it with great patience, even when they were busy with other things. I also appreciate their suggestions for some of the presidential items that appear in this book, as well as their help separating fact from fiction in some areas.

My thanks to historian and author Richard McElroy of the McKinley Museum and National Memorial in Canton for helping me confirm the story about McKinley's carnation, and for his many other suggestions for the book.

My appreciation to Cathi Baumgardner of the Ohio State Fair for tracking down the picture of the butter cow for me.

Longtime friends Ted and Karen Driscol of Lorain helped in the early stages of research with trips to the library and several suggestions.

Thanks also to Steve Goldurs, Bob Levkulich, and Matt Rafferty, longtime colleagues at Fox 8 TV who helped along the way, and especially to Cragg Eichman, Mark Saksa, Jimmy Holloway, Bob Wilkinson, Ralph Tarsitano, Gregg Lockhart, Roger Powell, Loren Kruse, Lisa March, Tomi Toyama-Ambrose, and Bill Wolfe for their assistance and for providing some of the pictures in this book.

As I write this I am aware that I have probably overlooked others who made valuable contributions to this book. My apologies to those I've forgotten—I hope you will remind me so that we can include you in future editions.

To be sure, it would be impossible to thank every single person who contributed to this book. There were literally hundreds, and I hope you all know that I am grateful for the help.

Finally, thank you to my family, who helped in so many ways.

ABOUT THE AUTHOR

Neil Zurcher logged more than a million miles on Ohio's roads over 25 years as a TV travel reporter. He was the original host of the "One Tank Trips" travel report, which aired on Cleveland television and has since been imitated in other television markets throughout the United States. Called "One of the most respected and knowledgeable travel writers in the state" by former Ohio governor George Voinovich, Zurcher received the Distinguished Service award from the Society of Professional Journalism and the Silver Circle award from the National Academy of Television Arts and Sciences. He has received an Award for Excellence in Broadcasting from the Cleveland Association of Broadcasters. He was also inducted into the Ohio Broadcasters Hall of Fame and received their "Living Legacy" award in 2007. He writes regularly for AAA *Ohio Motorist* magazine and the Cleveland *Plain Dealer* and has written five books about Ohio, including *Ohio Road Trips* and *Strange Tales from Ohio*.

DID I MISS SOMETHING?

Well, that's what third editions are for. If I left out your favorite Ohio Oddity, or if you know of someplace in the book that has changed, please let me know; I'll try to include it next time I update the book. Write to me at:

Ohio Oddities
c/o Gray & Company, Publishers
1588 E. 40th St.
Cleveland, OH 44103
email: ohiooddities@grayco.com

PHOTO CREDITS

Page 6, courtesy of the Circleville Pumpkin Show; p. 10, courtesy of the Ohio State Fair; p. 13, courtesy of the Dewberry Lawnmower Racing Team; p. 17, Lisa Kocher; p. 19 (left and right), courtesy of the Motts Military Museum; p. 23 (left and right), courtesy of the Marion County Historical Society; p. 25, courtesy of the *Marion Star*; p. 31, courtesy of the Ohio Division of Travel & Tourism; p. 32, courtesy of the Longaberger Company; p. 34, courtesy of the American Ceramic Society; p. 44, courtesy of the Rutherford B. Hayes Presidential Center; p. 49, courtesy of the Allen County Museum; p. 53, courtesy of the Ohio Division of Travel & Tourism; p. 63, courtesy of the Quaker Square Inn; p. 78, Dave Hopper; p. 79, courtesy of Wolf Timbers; p. 83, courtesy of the Library of Congress, Prints and Photographs Division; p. 86, courtesy of the Canton Classic Car Museum; p. 94, courtesy of the Cleveland Museum of Natural History; p. 97, courtesy of the Cleveland Police Historical Society; p. 99, courtesy of the Cleveland Police Historical Society; p. 119, William and Linda Cundiff; p. 125, courtesy of Kelleys Island State Park; p. 126, courtesy of the Kent State Fashion Museum; p. 127, courtesy of the Columbia Career Center; p. 147 (top), courtesy of the Hoover Historical Center; p. 147 (bottom), courtesy of the Allen County Museum; p. 149, Bonnie Zurcher; p. 153, Bonnie Zurcher; p. 155 (left), courtesy of the Seville Historical Society; p. 160, courtesy of the Twinsburg Twins Day Festival; p. 161, Dick Goddard; p. 163, Pete Perich; p. 166, courtesy of Vernon Craig; p. 168, courtesy of Vernon Craig; p. 173, courtesy of the Dickinson Cattle Company; p. 174, courtesy of the Dickinson Cattle Company; p. 183, courtesy of the New Straitsville Moonshine Festival; p. 184, courtesy of the Athens Count Convention and Visitors' Bureau; p. 192, Jim Rankin; p. 193, courtesy of Coney Island Park; p. 195, courtesy of the Preble County Pork Festival; p. 197, courtesy of the U.S. Air Force Museum; p. 199, courtesy of Jungle Jim's International Farmers Market; p. 201, courtesy of the Greenville/Darke County Conversation and Visitors' Bureau; p. 203, Melissa Luttman; p. 206, courtesy of Discover Ohio; p. 212, Roger Powell; p. 213, courtesy of the Seville Historical Society; p. 216, courtesy of the Pike County Convention and Visitors Bureau.

INDEX